The View from the Peak

The View
from the Peak

J.A. COLE

FABER AND FABER

London · Boston

First published in 1979
by Faber and Faber Limited
3 Queen Square London WC1N 3AU
Printed in Great Britain by
The Bowering Press Ltd Plymouth
All rights reserved

British Library Cataloguing in Publication Data

Cole, John Alfred
  The view from the peak.
  I. Woolwich, Eng.—Social life and customs
  I. Title
  942.1'62 DA690.W897

ISBN 0-571-11414-8

Contents

Foreword

This book is not an autobiography, except in the sense that all descriptive reporting is to some extent autobiographical. It is, rather, an attempt to assume the role of a rather specialized reporter covering the period between about 1907 and 1929. So far as I know, what is so prominent in my memory has not hitherto figured in childhood reminiscences. I shall add nothing to the sun-bonnets and daisy-chains scenes of the Edwardian age or to the cocktail-bar and dole-queue literature of the twenties. People born in similar surroundings to mine at about the same time may well protest that they scarcely recognize the neighbourhood, that it is a highly idiosyncratic account of a place and its people. Well, every descriptive writer has to run that risk. Yet there will be others, born in widely-scattered places, who will have not identical but parallel experiences.

Memory is, of course, subject to that secondary elaboration which sets in within half an hour of an occurrence, muddling up the scene, recasting the actors and revising the dialogue. In certain respects this awareness inhibits me. I mostly avoid direct speech because, with a few exceptions, I cannot recall the colloquialisms of my earliest years. One of the exceptions is 'all Sigarny', which people said where they would now say 'O.K.'. The expression derived from the early 1880s and was a tribute to that 'very model of a modern Major-General', Sir Garnet Wolseley. 'Au revoir' (in an anglicized pronunciation) was in vogue, and so was the word blasé. A halfpenny was known as a sou, a farthing a fiddler, and the magnificent five-shilling piece, the crown, was also called a dollar—a usage which still lingers as a sad reminder of what sterling once was. (When British currency was decimalized, a symbol of British stability and continuity was destroyed. Previously, century-old pennies were still circulating and valid. As a child I used to compare the different likenesses of Queen Victoria, ranging over sixty years, on a handful of pennies.) Catch-phrases, the repetition of which could cause helpless laughter, have become displaced in my memory so much that I could not confidently place them in the right decade.

But generations shared memories. An oral tradition of recounting personal histories was still strong; a child learnt its elders' stories by heart and could participate in their earlier lives; their reminiscences were listened to not only out of respect but with close interest. Again and again I experienced the heart-rending dismay of my paternal grandfather, Alfred, and his older brother, William, at the fate of their rocking-horse. Their father was a wood- and ivory-turner; a steady contract with a brewery for wooden taps for casks provided the bread and butter, but his pride was in the chessmen and ornamental furniture he produced; a card in his shop window read: 'Instruction Given To Amateurs'. For his sons he carved a superb rocking-horse; even as old men their eyes grew round in admiration of his craftsmanship. It became, however, a source of contention between the two boys. As soon as one wanted to ride it the other claimed it. Repeatedly their father warned them that he would not tolerate quarrels over it. One day, without a word, he interrupted a dispute, carried the toy into his workshop and chopped it up.

William related the most gruesome story. While on a business trip to London from Rochester, where he had a sports goods shop, he saw pirates' bodies hanging from a gallows after their public execution. The scene was like a fair, he said, with hawkers shouting and a high-spirited crowd surging about; people walked beneath the gallows and those who were tall enough reached up and struck the dead men's boots, causing—amid laughter—the bodies to spin. That eye-witness detail of the boots permanently fixed the story in my mind.

His nephew, my uncle, was sharply observant and had a narrative gift. I can see, as he saw them, chained convicts working in Portsmouth Dockyard, and feel the dew on iron basement railings as, a young apprentice, he ran down a steep hill on dark winter mornings to the workshop whose lights twinkled mistily below. His favourite recital, however, was a news story of his youth. Standing on a vantage point known locally as the Peak, pointing his walking stick in a direction some distance up the Thames, he would say: 'That's where the *Princess Alice* went down.' After a short, thoughtful pause he would begin. He spoke with feeling, and the tale never bored me. Recently I looked up an account of this accident, and I was surprised at how few details were missing in my memory. My uncle had been ten years old at the time, and in no way involved, yet he had absorbed the newspaper reports and the excited conversations. On a September evening in 1878 a small passenger paddle steamer was proceeding up-river towards London Bridge, packed with passengers. In Galleons Reach (it was exciting to hear that name pronounced—it is a stretch between Woolwich and Barking) it was struck amidships by a large vessel, the *Bywell Castle*, and sank within four minutes. Over six hundred passengers lost their lives.

This tragedy had not then been superseded in the memory by greater or more spectacular events. From the same spot it would be possible to point in a different direction and say: 'That's where the Zeppelin came down in flames at Cuffley in September 1916.' Does anybody stand there and recall it now? Other conflagrations have occurred meanwhile. My elders had not lived on the other side of a great divide; no equivalents existed of such phrases as 'before the First World War' or 'up to the outbreak of the Second World War'.

Anecdotal history was supplemented for me not by published memoirs or child's simplified histories but by nineteenth-century journalism. Incentives to learn to read were powerful; apart from toys and puzzles, no other indoor diversion was available. Houses were silent except for the ticking and striking of clocks. Meals were separated by aeons of time. By the age of five I was heavily addicted to print. The spare bedroom contained a wardrobe stuffed with old magazines, some of them bound in volumes and going back for decades. When my parents set up house together, they must have brought with them every periodical they had ever inherited from their elders or bought themselves, and they were still bringing this museum up to date. Somebody when ill might want something to read, my mother would say as she added to the swaying stacks of paper. She was right. They proved a solace through my childish illnesses, and incidentally introduced me to Dickens and Conan Doyle. The characters in *Harmsworth's*, the *Strand Magazine*, the *Boy's Own Paper* and *The Lady's World* lived again for me. The ladies were involved in the cycling craze of the nineties; wearing straw boaters, high-necked, square-shouldered blouses and ankle-length skirts, they were drawn posing beside oddly flexible-looking bicycles. Top-hatted men hailed hansoms, horse-cab conductors leaned, arms wide, from their platforms to assist passengers, soldiers in tropical kit waved goodbye from trains, robins perched on holly branches on the covers of Christmas numbers, Dr Gordon-Stables offered manly advice to eager boys, Spofforth was bowling and Persimmon winning

[9]

the Derby. There were, too, the murderers, sketched unsympatheti-
cally in the dock by artists who attended the trials; faced by a judge of
superhuman majesty, flanked by grave warders, stared at unflinch-
ingly by counsel and jury, the accused was an isolated symbol of
evil confronted by justice. Artists also illustrated what they had not
seen : the murderer at the moment of striking a fatal blow, suffering
nightmares in the condemned cell, being addressed by the chaplain,
standing trussed on the trapdoor.

Thus the news stories of the previous twenty or thirty years were
as familiar to me as though I had lived through the period; my
elders were not strange beings left over from an era of comic clothes,
ridiculous conventions and general unenlightenment. Because of this
closeness, I can describe public events which occurred when I was
too young to remember them. In some respects the adult world was
very near; but in others the distance between adults and children
was unbridgeable. Children lived with the awareness of an adult world
surrounding them about which they were not supposed to betray
the slightest curiosity, and that barrier between adults and children
was only one of several. Each home was surrounded by a security
cordon; the people I describe were not, like the lowest social stratum,
accustomed to being studied as if they were a bee colony. A team of
anthropologists who, instead of sailing from Tilbury for some Pacific
island, had taken a suburban train from London and camped in the
woods where this book opens would have found their investigatory
techniques unrewarding. Outrage would have been the inhabitants'
reaction to questions covering their source of livelihood, property,
relationships and personal behaviour. Head-hunters would have been
more co-operative, witch-doctors less secretive.

So in writing this book I am conscious of doing something of
which the characters concerned would have disapproved. In a curious
flash of precognition my uncle (the one who related the *Princess
Alice* story) asked me never to publish anything about our family.
'Your grandfather', he said, 'would not have liked it.' At that time
he had no reason to suppose that I would ever publish a line on any
subject, but he issued this notice that everything he said was classified Confidential just to be sure. I have broken the embargo, but I
have compromised. I do not name the Estate (which, I must emphasize at the start, was not a council estate) where much of the
action takes place, and I do not want to do so because, although
topographically it is easily identifiable, in the sense in which I des-

cribe it it no longer exists. For a time it existed as an entity in some people's minds; no doubt each one of them saw it differently. I concentrate largely on a few personalities, but it was a concept to many more. To how many more? I could not guess, but numbers do not matter. What proportion of the ratepayers of Bloomsbury and Chelsea helped to form the character associated with those names?

Survivors, who grew up in the same strict tradition of keeping themselves to themselves, will understand why I have not given the characters their full names. If I were to I should have to write in the panegyric style of an obituary notice. As persons are here presented, they can be recognized or disclaimed, as anyone pleases. It is a pity that some will not receive tributes which are their due; on the other hand, if I were confined to a recital of good deeds I should have to miss out other characters who balance the record.

One odd experience, arising from having grown up on the Estate, was to discover that what seemed to me everyday topics, long worn into clichés, were in other circles regarded as novel and revolutionary. In fact, theories which my elders took for granted are now shouted in slogan form as though they derive from a recent revelation. Ideas and fantasies were so much part of my youthful experience that they seem, in retrospect, more real than events. I might have started with a recollection of picking bluebells in a local wood; instead, a different scene in that wood clamours to be recorded.

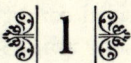

1

Faint in the East

The Countess of Warwick smiled at me one afternoon in the summer of 1907. Name-dropping in this reportage ends with the Countess and there will be no recollections of fashionable garden-parties on immaculate lawns or weekend conferences of tweedy Fabians. She is introduced only because her presence sets the period and tells us something about the community on which, in an early motor car (cars were as rare as titled ladies in the district), she fleetingly descended.

We were in a clearing in a wood on the boundary between London and Kent and she was making a speech to inaugurate an open-air day school. Her audience laughed at my exuberant cry on suddenly, from the height of my father's shoulder, having a view over the heads of the crowd. A public speaker cannot ignore that kind of innocent interruption, but must appear to enjoy it as much as everybody else. The Countess's smile, which no doubt merited the adjective 'gracious', and the patient pause while the toddler was hushed and attention returned to the platform seem to have enveloped the gathering in a warm feeling of shared humanity. Not very much of note ever occurred in the locality, so trivial incidents tended to form the substance of much-repeated anecdotes. Whenever, in later years, Lady Warwick's name appeared in the newspapers, or open-air schools were discussed, the story was revived by my mother, and its details became so familiar that I was almost persuaded that I could remember the occasion myself.

Other people, who seemed to have forgotten my intervention in the proceedings, were also apt, even years later, to recall that afternoon for no other reason than that they had heard a countess *speak*. In those pre-broadcasting days they seldom heard the speech of people far removed from their own class. Her tone and pronunciation, the rhythm of her sentences, were alien and fascinating to them; to them she was scarcely more natural than would have been an actress playing the role of a society lady. When professing to quote her, they did so in the kind of speech adopted by foppish characters, with names like Lord Algy, in touring companies' farces, pantomime barons and monocled concert-party comedians. Normally the vicar provided what was thought to be cultured English; he was far outclassed by the Countess.

But it was not, it must be said, one of those occasions when an illustrious person appears to perform an opening ceremony of some institution of which she knows practically nothing and reads a speech written by somebody else. Lady Warwick was herself an educational innovator, she was a member of a board of guardians, and she had taken the trouble to visit and do something about the rural poor. In inviting her, of course, the sponsors of the open-air school had reckoned less on her experience of social work than on her notoriety to get them press coverage and a substantial crowd. At that time she was the Labour movement's most exotic advocate. The *Daily Mirror*, not then a popularizer of progressive views, crossly called her 'a freak attraction' in referring to her appearances at public meetings. Of course people were curious to see her, and they knew that somewhere in her background lay a scandal, although, I suspect, they were uncertain what it was about—the common remark was that 'someone at the Court offended her'. It is a moot point whether, had they been better informed, they would have been more shocked by her amours or by her debts. Of course there was a good deal of jostling among local men in public life, and their wives, for the privilege of sitting on the patform while she addressed the crowd or, failing that, of being presented. But there was another, and possibly a stronger, reason for the interest in her. A good proportion of those who were gratified by her presence were conscious of holding minority political views; they saw themselves as pioneers of a new moral force in politics. Their feeling that the Labour movement was a moral and not merely a political and industrial force was fortified when it attracted advocates who had nothing to gain materially from its success, but who would suffer financial and social disadvantages from a transformation of society. Deserters from the other side were few.

That open-air school was one sign of the century's bright promise. Everybody knew that everything was sure to get better and better; the important thing was to make a start, however humble. The sponsors had not been deterred when the London County Council lacked legal authority to grant money for such a school. They sought a practical solution by their own efforts. It did not cross their minds that worthy causes can be promoted by shouting slogans outside the council chamber and scuffling with the police. Funds were raised by voluntary contributions, as a matter of course the parents paid for the children's food, and the local co-operative society lent the woods rent-free.

Do not imagine a school with verandas, sliding glass doors, day beds, ingenious toys. A jungle missionary-school could not have been more simply equipped, yet it could not have been founded with more zeal and optimism. Its purpose was to provide an open-air life for some sixty children suffering from chest complaints; it provided the fresh air, some instruction and very little else. Shelter was supplied by a rustic shed, with a rudimentary kitchen at the rear. The children sat on forms at trestle-tables. A photograph taken of their recreation ground, an area of coarse grass, shows them at what was then called drill, deployed in seven long ranks, their arms rather limply extended sidewards as they keep still for the exposure. The boys are dressed in a variety of clothing—jerseys, sailor blouses, Norfolk jackets with Eton collars, knee-length shorts, breeches buttoned below the knee, stockings and boots. The girls wear calf-length white pinafores with black stockings and boots. With her back to the camera, and facing the children, is a nurse with a head-dress flowing to her waist, a tiny cape, sleeves ending in cuffs at the wrists, an ankle-length skirt which falls in folds like a heavy curtain, and a long white apron. Her outstretched arms are straight and tense; even from the rear her commanding presence is evident. The children are being observed from the sides and the back by two male teachers and one female (the men in suits and tall white collars, the woman in a full-length black dress and a white apron) who have the taut watchfulness of sheepdogs and who will, on detecting the slightest wobble, emit a warning bark. This description does not imply that their attitude to the children was other than kindly; they were simply fulfilling their role as adults who, when dealing with children, were expected to behave like an army of occupation in a territory where the natives were unreliable. Something in the children's attitude is characteristic of the period, and it is not wholly explained by the necessity to adopt a rigid posture while being photographed, by the pathetic unsuitability of their clothing for physical exercise, or their being a selected group of what were then called 'delicate' children. They are slightly hunched, as though there has just been a clap of thunder and they are expecting an immediate downpour; what they are constantly anticipating is a reproof, however hard they strive to do the right thing. Not that they would have thought there was anything sad about the picture. The day the photographer came would have been an event—photography still had a faint aura of magic. The weather would have been watched with anxiety—the sun shone—and the prints displayed on mantelpieces, pianos, sideboards and what-nots for years.

The Countess's audience, which included the public-spirited elect of the neighbourhood, people who sat on committees, councillors, teachers, civil servants and—the dominant class in the locality—skilled engineering workers with their families, heard her describe German open-air schools as the model. Perhaps, in doing so, she intended to undermine a common assumption that Germany was a naval, military and commercial menace by drawing attention to Germany as a pioneer of social legislation. I doubt, however, whether she would have dented their conviction that nobody anywhere could have been more progressive than they were, although they would have listened respectfully. The French coast was about seventy miles from where they were assembled, but only a few had ever been out of England; to them, life in foreign countries must be merely an inferior version of their own. The unshakeable confidence of the upper classes permeated all social levels. Lady Warwick concluded, in formal fashion, by expressing the conviction that the school would be a success and the precursor of many others.

No one seems to have recorded any medical evidence about an improvement in the children's health, but they should have been toughened by the experience. Pre-1914 summers evoke visions of cloudless skies, straw hats, blazers and parasols. That summer was an exception. Any of the delicate children of 1907 who have survived will not have forgotten how they often huddled under the rustic shed while rain swept in and splashed their exercise books, and how during drill they slithered about on the sodden grass. The weather's interruptions to the routine were probably welcomed by the pupils as a diversion which emphasized the difference from ordinary school. The school ran through its scheduled course until October. The optimists were ultimately justified, as they had never doubted that they would be. The London County Council recognized its success and adopted the idea.

But this educational venture, despite its distinguished patronage, was merely a minor skirmish in a long-term campaign. Another aspect of it could be observed annually, in the same woods, during an event advertised, misleadingly, as a 'Grand Fête and Gala'. Socially, the summer season opened and closed with it.

An event of this sort belongs to the youthful recollections of many people—the flower show, and the emotional strain experienced by gardeners bringing blooms on or holding them back; the anxious women, reproaching themselves for their temerity in promising to enter cake- and jam-making competitions; the volunteer refreshment-servers who at the eleventh hour are called away to nurse sick relatives; the excitement of watching men erect a marquee; the gloomy speculations about the weather. But this was not the usual rural garden-party; it had a purpose beyond any local charity.

The procession, led by somebody's uniformed 'silver prize band', assembled a couple of miles away and, such was the penetrating power of wind instruments and drums in the quiet streets, the music could be heard over the whole of its route. The bandsmen marched in military style, and the demonstrators following, although less disciplined, did their best to keep step. No policemen accompanied them to prevent disorder, and the marchers must not be imagined as protesting that they were downtrodden; dressed in their best, starched white collars gleaming, boots reflecting the sun, wearing smart straw or panama hats or well-brushed bowlers, shaved as closely as soldiers on parade, they were celebrating their respectability and prosperity, triumphantly proclaiming their privileged involvement in the crafts and mysteries illustrated, with a wealth of allegorical fantasy, on their banners. Those banners, carried by red-faced, anxious men who braced themselves against gusts of wind, recalled the solemn pride of medieval craft guilds, the element of freemasonry in early combinations of workmen, the Victorian worship of railways, steamships and heavy industry, the concept of Britain as 'the workshop of the world'. Sturdy artisans, their shirt-sleeves rolled up, shook hands over anvils or posed leaning on sledge-hammers. Angelic figures personified unity, co-operation and brotherly love. Sometimes a cartload of children followed, drawn by immaculate horses decorated with sparkling brasses and coloured ribbons, the driver as smart as if he had been taking a four-in-hand to Ascot, and the cart scrubbed so that no summer frock should suffer a smudge.

Two panama-hatted men sat at a trestle-table in the gateway to the woods. One took the admission money—threepence—and the

[17]

other tore a ticket off a perforated roll. Behind them was the cool, dark wood, flecked with patches of sunlight, and at the end of a path an open space where stood a marquee and figures could be seen moving about. Having bought their tickets, people quickened their pace in case they missed some event.

The band, still playing, marched through the gates and straight to the circles of chairs and music-stands awaiting them. After sorting out music and conferring with the players, the white-gloved conductor, with an air of immense authority, stepped on to a box and raised his baton. Throughout the afternoon the music thrillingly filled the woods and floated over the Estate.

In the refreshment shed which had once housed the open-air school women in long white aprons stood behind paper-covered trestle-tables and, with more than a hint of condescension in their manner, served urn-made tea, jam or bloater-paste sandwiches (made of newly-baked white bread), slab fruit-cake, biscuits, minerals, ice-cream and sweets. They were 'giving their services' and very conscious of serving a cause.

An initiated observer would here have detected a difference between this event and all the other apparently similar gatherings on village greens and in the grounds of grand houses. Many customers were noting the brand of tea being served, the makers' names on the sweet-jars, biscuit-tins and bottles of minerals, not to check the prices but to ensure that trade with the capitalist world was reduced to an unavoidable minimum. Unacceptable items could later be the subject of angry debates and indignant resolutions.

The marquee housed a fruit and vegetable show. Here, in the diffused light under the canvas, voices were lowered, perhaps out of awareness that the annual ceremony of a cult was in progress. Passions which in other communities were inspired by racing pigeons, whippets, horses, football, golf or bridge were here concentrated on such endeavours as producing the most exquisite Frau Karl von Druschki ever seen in the district. Straw-hatted, pipe-smoking visitors moved slowly between the exhibits, non-committally contemplating the cosseted blooms and the unnaturally uniform vegetables. Conscious that critical eyes were lingering over their Firsts, Seconds, Thirds and Highly Commendeds, the judges sat by themselves, murmuring gravely over catalogues.

Some rather casually organized races for children took place, and aroused little attention from the adults, for whom the afternoon was another Sunday-type promenade which happened to be held on a Saturday. Dressed up for the occasion, they were determined to get in as much gossiping and baby-inspecting as time allowed.

At about this stage a couple advanced into the woods, he smiling and hat-raising, she smiling and bowing, like the squire and his lady emerging from the big house to meet the villagers. Occasionally their slow progress was halted when they stopped, shook hands, chatted and laughed. Although he, Walter, responded affably and even with style to the greetings from all sides, he seemed to want to make himself even smaller and thinner than he was by shrinking into himself. His steely eyes looked warily through gold-rimmed spectacles, his Kitchener-type moustache gave his pinched face a touch of sadness; with his thick dark hair combed upwards in a quiff he might, in his weekday attire of tall collar and black tail-coat, have served 'Phiz' as a model of a hungry usher. To the fête he wore a straw hat and a light-grey suit but, like all the men, he retained his tall collar. Jane, his wife, was a fine figure of a woman, as the phrase then went; taller and broader than Walter, round-faced and healthily pink, chestnut-haired, wearing a complicated accumulation of garments which swirled and fluttered, wielding a parasol, she was an imposing sight, a type designed by nature to present school prizes and declare ante-natal clinics open. Far from shrinking, she expanded, drawing lesser people into her orbit; by the time they reached the marquee she and Walter had acquired a group of attendants. This reception, quite unsought, was accorded them as local personalities.

A different concert party was engaged each year, but they were invariably either 'nigger minstrels' (no inhibition about the name) or pierrots (pleasantly associated with seaside entertainment; a well-worn contemporary joke was that a pierrot is a man who talks rot on a pier). The 'niggers' were, of course, white men, which was a pity as black men might have introduced the enchantment of rag-time. 'Plantation songs', sung as though conducted in strict tempo by the local choir-mistress, a banjo, the bones, and anecdotes about chicken-stealing coons (mostly named Rastus) projected the Deep South to this audience of allotment-holders and their wives and children. Oddly enough, the pierrots' make-up, with its stark white and dark shading, looked more exotic than the burnt cork. The day-light and the faint stage-lighting were unkind to the performers, viewed as they were at too-close range by men who never saw make-up in their daily lives and by women who would never have dared

[19]

to use it. Their upright piano, maltreated by frequent exposure to the open air, was almost inaudible beyond a few yards, and not many of the singers succeeded in making themselves heard by people standing behind the seated audience. 'If you don't get near the front you won't hear the words,' people warned each other; most of the audience were resigned to not hearing 'the words' in full, but entertainments were so rare that they would not miss a minute of whatever was available.

Then came the interval and the speeches. The audience was kept captive by the knowledge that seats vacated would be immediately taken and occupied during the second part of the concert. A wooden table was carried on to the stage, a committee—in their best suits but hatless—filed in and sat in a semi-circle facing the audience. The chairman and the speaker followed, also hatless. The unwritten convention seemed to be that the men on the stage, which was covered at the top and sides, were practically indoors, and that any-way it was a courtesy to the audience to be bareheaded. It was an obsessively hat-wearing age, however, and men who that afternoon had been nervous of sunstroke were now, that evening, fearing a chill. In the audience their wives listened anxiously as speakers who appeared about to go into a peroration embarked on another subject, thus prolonging the meeting and postponing the time when hats could be resumed.

Speeches were a ritual. Most speakers had accumulated a sequence of clichés which they delivered whatever the occasion. As they talked, their brains were scarcely working; they were shouting into the space before them, exercising no more mental effort than a child reciting a familiar poem. The audience were part of the ritual; they recognized the sentiments, nodded at emotive phrases, clapped as the recital ended. The message of the preliminary speakers, if a meaning could be disentangled from the welter of words, was loyalty to whatever interest the speaker represented: put the cross on the ballot paper in the right place, join your trade union, shop at the co-operative stores, remember your duty to the great working-class movement. By the time I was twelve, having a good verbal memory, I could have made any of these speeches myself. Blindfolded, I could have identified any local speaker and finished his sentences for him.

The chief speaker was seldom such a draw as Lady Warwick but he was usually a 'name', perhaps a Member of Parliament, a prospective candidate, or a trade-union organizer, and therefore a man who had to think of his career even at the risk of catching cold. His prime qualification was a powerful voice. Unaided by any amplification device, speakers got their training by competing in market squares on Saturday evenings against the noise of barking stall-holders, screaming children, indifferent shopping crowds, Salvation Army services, and horses' hooves. What they actually said was of scant importance compared with their ability to bellow tirelessly. The style that emerged was messianic. They sounded like revivalist preachers, which indeed some of them had been, and their message was a vague one of deliverance from evil oppressors, and future glory on earth. Surprisingly, considering the audience's quiet respectability, they preferred agitators to lecturers, and the more ranting the performance the greater the applause.

The concert party, with a routine no less standardized than that of the speakers who had filled in the interval, reappeared for another hour or so. In the background, as twilight fell and coloured lights were switched on in the trees, the flower show was dismantled and its heavier props loaded on a van. The horse, cropping the grass while waiting, twitched slightly in response to the pattings and strokings of onlookers. The concreted space where the spectators had sat was cleared for dancing, and, back from a pub just outside the Estate's boundaries, the silver prize band, its instruments reflecting the lights, blew tentative grunts and trills.

Dancing was under the command (no other expression would be adequate) of a master of ceremonies, who had the voice and moustache of a sergeant-major and whose white suit and panama hat gave him a colonial air. He was at his most impressive when calling the figures of The Lancers. Dancers were ordered into their positions with a jovial ferocity and sharply corrected if they made mistakes. He never actually bawled 'As you were!' but, with an anguished cry and a signal to the conductor, he would stop dancers and band if a set made a false start, and give some staccato instructions before the square-bashing was allowed to continue. Nobody resented this discipline or thought it inappropriate to a festive occasion, and the local newspaper's reference to 'the ever-popular M.C.' was no exaggeration.

Prominent among the dancers was Jane, who functioned as an unofficial assistant to the M.C. Her set never went wrong in The Lancers; she had them welded into a disciplined unit from the start.

[21]

A good dancer herself, she was seldom to be seen dancing with a practised partner; her sense of duty compelled her to seize, literally, any diffident young man she saw standing on the edge of the dancing space and teach him to dance. Such was her momentum, so firm her embrace, and so emphatic her instructions (her lips could be seen moving as she counted), that her pupil could do nothing but surrender himself to the movement. No other woman but Jane could have behaved in this way and escaped gossip; she had the gift of being friendly, even of looking and sounding affectionate, while being impersonal; it would have been unthinkable to suspect her of flirting. She was an institution dedicated to laudable aims, one of which was 'to bring people out'.

At half-past ten the final order, 'Take your partners for the last waltz!' brought missing couples out of the dark woods. The M.C., now abdicating, danced with his wife, and waved graceful thanks to the musicians, who switched to a hurried version of *Auld Lang Syne*—a curious practice for the south of England, as nobody ever learnt the words and would not have understood them if they had. Glowing with exertion and benevolence, Jane rejoined Walter who, flat-footed and with little sense of rhythm, refused even to try to dance. Around him were half a dozen committee-type men. Someone would remark that they had better go home before they were eaten by gnats, somebody else would say well, it was over for another year, and they would join the throng moving out of the gate.

The band's departure lacked the pomp of their arrival. Even before the lights in the wood had been turned out, they had made their way through the gas-lit, tree-lined streets back to The Harrow Arms, where they were joined by the more independent male members of their audiences. But most people hurried home, and by eleven they were drinking hot milk or cocoa, eating biscuits, or finishing a bottle of stout with cheese and pickles, fondling the dogs which, if left at home, had given them a rapturous welcome, and nursing purring cats. Children were hustled to bed before the rebelliousness induced by so much festivity exploded into temper tantrums. While the parents were alert for signs of obstreperousness, children were equally watchful for the irritability which they associated with all authority; however tranquil and cosy these little households seemed, emotional outbursts were never far below the surface.

However, it would have been a day giving little cause for regret. Despite the revolutionary tone of the speech, nobody became sufficiently inflamed to shake a fist or shout a slogan; nobody ended up in a police-station cell or suffered a hangover on Sunday morning. If there were any regrets they concerned some minor social *faux pas*— a failure to acknowledge adequately a neighbour's greeting, an incautious remark about somebody's dress, age, front-room curtains or children's behaviour.

One of the reporters present, William Henry, concentrated on the names of those on the platform, noting with particular care the J.P.s, aldermen and councillors, types liable to be affronted if their names appeared in print without these distinctions. He represented an 'official organ', which position obliged him to attend certain functions whether or not they had any news value. When he sat at the back of the platform taking a note he added prestige to the occasion; people nudged each other and said: 'A reporter'. The other reporter concentrated on the flower-show winners; his paper called itself 'independent' (a euphemism for Conservative) and he was present only because the co-operative society was an advertiser. Any comment he made concerned the weather; either the sun smiled on the occasion or rain fell but failed to damp the spirits of those present. To both men, it would be safe to assume, the event was a bore. Yet the locality, the wood where the fête and gala took place and the Estate where most of those attending it lived, provided a story which peculiarly belonged to their time.

All that ground had, up to 1535, belonged to the Dukes of Suffolk. In 1720 it came into the possession of a charitable society whose object was the conversion of North American Indians. American independence led to others taking over the task of converting Red Indians, or of reducing their numbers to manageable proportions, and the Charity Commissioners acquired the society's assets. Right at the end of the nineteenth century, when the strongly flowing stream of progress looked like becoming a flood in the twentieth century, another society—not religious or philanthropic but healthily viable and independent—bought the two farms of which the property then consisted. Since that time the society had, terrace by terrace, developed the Estate, with its own funds and employing its own builders. The houses had been sold on 99-year leases to the residents, who thus came to form part of the ten per cent of the country's population who then owned their own houses. Apart from their house-ownership, they were shareholders—and very consciously so—in the society owning the land. Thus, individually, they were house-owners, and collectively landlords. All this had been achieved by normal legal processes and their title deeds were unquestionable. Not a penny in subsidy was received from local or national government; no processions demanded expropriation; no mob threatened bailiffs; no squatters invaded the area. By an entirely constitutional process the land once owned by Dukes was transferred to the People. Many of the participants in this peaceful takeover had been unaware of its significance, but a minority saw its revolutionary potential as well as its practical advantages; it was they who gave the Estate its distinctive character, who provided the story.

2

The View from the Peak

Like Aristotle's ideal city state, the entire Estate could be viewed from a hilltop. Locally this eminence was known as the Peak, a name not to be found on maps. Many places have a peak; this one did not fit the *Concise Oxford Dictionary's* definition as a 'pointed tops esp. of mountain', but the word described the feeling of being there. The Estate was at river level; behind it the land rose sharply to an extensive wooded area called the heath, about three hundred feet above sea level. This modest elevation which was the Peak was high enough to provide an exciting view across the marshland, river, the county of Essex, and London, with the silhouettes of St Paul's Cathedral and Tower Bridge dominating all other buildings and challenged only by the cranes drooping over ships in the busy docks.

'Shall we climb up to the Peak?' my mother would ask, as though suggesting an expedition with ropes and picks. To me the climb offered all the thrills of an expedition. The grandeur and savagery of nature have never been more evident to me than on the sandy track which provided the most direct route to the Peak. Rainwater had cut gorges through it, and after a heavy fall these were the channels for a swift torrent of yellow water whirling twigs and leaves along with it and grinding the underlying gravel. The banks of these narrow cuttings would have been no more than a foot deep, but to a child they were awesome evidence of the power of natural forces. On reaching level ground the flood spread out into pools on the edge of the Estate, to be negotiated only by jumping across a series of sandy islands. No alpine scenery could have given greater aesthetic satisfaction than the spectacle of this water tumbling down to the plain. No canoe race over rapids could have afforded more excitement than the progress of two matchsticks launched into the stream near the top and followed in their hazardous voyage.

Adults used to complain of the state of the path even when it was dry. 'You could twist your ankle in those ruts.' Sometimes it was repaired with a load of stones and earth; nature soon took over again, with a spectacular flood—just a heavy shower was enough—

and those who wanted to keep their boots clean or had perambulators to push were compelled to go at least three times the distance by road to reach the Peak from another direction.

Yet despite its treacherous surface, on a sunny summer afternoon before the Great War the Peak was the route most favoured by family parties heading for the heath and the Sunday parade. The ceremony of the promenade required formidable preparations from the polishing of boots to the brushing of hats—as late as 1912 the more dignified mechanics were still walking out in the top hats they had worn at their weddings. On all but the hottest days, formal suits of the best and warmest materials were put on, and children were warned of the dangers of leaving off a single layer of clothing. 'The sun may be shining but there's a very cool breeze.' Women put their hats on an hour before they were due to start, plunging long hatpins into them and into their thickly-coiled hair with movements suggesting a conjuror pushing long knives into a box supposed to contain his sequined assistant. Tight gloves were cautiously rolled on and then, the final act before departure, the veil was pulled down over the face. Perceiving these welcome activities, dogs endured agonies of waiting. They curled up and appeared to be asleep except for their flicking ears, they opened their eyes and raised their heads expectantly if anyone approached the front door, they ran around whimpering and sometimes, in an endeavour to hurry things along, they snatched their collars and leads from the hat-stand and offered them to anyone known to be sympathetic. Tempers rose with the tension; when they ultimately started, children were subdued and adults apparently near to exhaustion. In contrast, the dogs were quiveringly alert; their friendliness towards other dogs and people not infrequently caused owners to stop and chat.

The adults gasped their way up the incline, taking frequent pauses. Perhaps, carrying the same weight of clothing, present-day adults would find the climb just as exhausting, but I suspect that they were playing a role which cast them as middle-aged at thirty and old at fifty. Age they drew to themselves as though they were putting on a cloak. Youthful looks in a person beyond first youth did not attract admiration. 'Mutton dressed as lamb' was a ready sneer and a much feared one. 'I can't wear that,' a customer would say to a shop assistant. 'It makes me look too young.' Make-up was not used at all; sometimes, with explanations that they had 'caught the sun' or been 'chafed by the wind', women would cautiously apply cold cream and powder but this was merely, as they said, to 'preserve the skin' and not to deceive. Hair-dyes were advertised widely, so presumably they had a sale, but deep shame attended their use and a woman known to dye her hair was marked down as a doubtful character. The users also ran the risk, because dyes were unreliable, of being branded for months with unnatural colours such as green or bright ginger. Men, too, were expected at an early age to attain a mature dignity; their photographs show them, still in their twenties, setting their features magisterially and leaning on walking-sticks. Even when in groups they refrained from 'larking about'; scuffling, pushing, shouting were the mark of louts, and especially of those from 'over the water' (the water was the river, and the real east end of London was considered to be on the northern side). They cultivated grave deliberate habits; ask one a question, or solicit his opinion, and you had to wait for a reply while he slowly shredded out tobacco from a pouch, stuffed it into his pipe, passed a lighted match across the bowl, drew in his cheeks and looked thoughtfully into the distance. The performance was both funny and exasperating (after it ceased to be impressive) but it was understandable; most of them had left school at fourteen and entered a world of contemptuous elders where the best defence was to grow up quickly; by their mid-twenties they had been in a pitiless working world for ten years. At twelve, or even younger, girls were accustomed to controlling younger children in an authoritative manner. It was not, therefore, to be expected that they would bound up to the Peak and demonstrate to the neighbourhood that they were really just very young men and women.

Like mountain climbers, people ascending to the Peak went through successive zones after leaving the shining new houses of the Estate. The path ran for a short distance between back-garden fences, and then came a belt of cultivated land: the allotments—a source of absorbing interest to the walkers, who knew the tenants of each piece and followed the progress of their crops week by week. Even I, still holding my father's hand, used to feel a tinge of worry about the blackfly infesting Mr Larkin's broad beans. The tenants, emulating their cottager forebears, had utilized their space so intensively that they wobbled like tightrope-walkers as they made their way along narrow ridges of earth to reach the centre of the patch and the tiny tarred sheds. Combined with their gardens, they had enough land to keep their families supplied with vegetables for most of the

year, with redcurrants and blackcurrants, gooseberries, and straw-
berries, to produce exhibits for the annual flower and vegetable show
and to ensure that the church was worthily decorated for the harvest
festival service. But they shared with anglers another advantage.
The allotments were some distance from their houses and therefore
out of the sight and sound of irritable women, fretful children and
violin and piano practice. Where men higher up the social scale
escaped domesticity by going to clubs, these men hurried to their
allotments. Certainly they worked hard there but they could also
spend hours sitting on a box outside a toolshed, smoking a pipe and
drinking beer, reading a paper and exchanging greetings with fellow
refugees. On their return home they were immune from criticism
by wives normally anxious to prove that a woman's lot was harder
than a man's; it was axiomatic that no man was better employed
than on his allotment.

The next zone, past the allotments, was divided by the path. On
the east side an apple orchard, declining into senility, symbolized
the gradual retreat of the county of Kent before London suburbia.
On the west side was a field of tall grass, a fearsome place because
snakes were sometimes glimpsed there. Then came a belt of thickly
growing trees and holly bushes, where walkers paused gratefully in
the shade before the final assault on the Peak up pine-log steps—
women twitched at their skirts with one hand and, giggling, held out
the other hand to their escorts who had already mounted to the
step above. Everybody lingered at the top to survey the scene.

When Mr Charlesworth, the vicar, boomed out the sentence: 'The
devil taketh him up into an exceeding high mountain, and
sheweth him all the kingdoms of the world, and the glory of
them,' I used to think of the view from the Peak. Actually, for the
purpose of demonstrating the world's activities, a lower level has
advantages over a mountain. The prospect from the Peak throbbed
with life, from the picturesque to the menacing. Cutting a broad
band across the landscape was the river, and on this moved, with a
dreamlike smoothness, the red-sailed Thames barges, carrying cargoes
to and from London. Sailing ships, and especially these bulky working boats, seemed to be propelled by an unfailing power; no one
could explain to me understandably how they moved in opposite
directions—from our angle and distance they could not be seen
tacking. They dominated the scene. The steamships I most clearly
remember are the magnificent Belle paddle-steamers of the General

Steam Navigation Company. Dressed with bright pennants, glittering and shining with brass and paint, their huge paddles churning the water into white tracks, they had for the untravelled watchers from the Peak the majesty of ocean liners in their stately progress towards Margate, Ramsgate, Clacton and Yarmouth. Most of them called at Southend too, but for people on the south side of the river the name lacked magic; Southend was regarded as in the Thames estuary and as being pretentious in calling itself Southend-on-Sea. The Edwardian artisan, trained to standards of perfection in his work, was anxious not to be fobbed off with an inferior article. In the concert-party comedian's patter Southend—usually referred to as Southend-on-Mud—was good for an automatic laugh, as were Tooting, Wigan and any Welsh place name beginning with Llan. Men with telescopes on the Southend promenade were alleged to offer a view of the sea for a penny, and would-be suicides who had paid to go to the end of the pier were said to demand their money back.

The river marked the border between Kent and Essex. It was a moment of delight when I learned that Essex was the land of the East Saxons; the scene over there—the smoke trails of railway engines, the colours of fields changing with the seasons—acquired the fascination of the foreign. The greens, browns and yellows of agriculture gave way to the west to the indistinct mass of London, perpetually hazy under the smoke, but in the middle-distance was an object of constant interest, the bright-red powder hulk moored in the river. It might have been placed squarely in the centre of the landscape to symbolize the local industry. Rumour asserted that this squat barge held enough explosive to devastate the entire area; those who believed this—and their number certainly included all the children—were thus accustomed, decades before the advent of the atomic bomb, to living under the threat of annihilation, an experience they seemed to find stimulating rather than worrying. The powder hulk's reminder of what power is all about was reinforced between 1910 and 1912 by the sight, a little further up the river, of a 'Dreadnought' under construction at the Thames Ironworks.

The *Thunderer*'s pink hull, with its overall length of 584 feet, could be seen for miles around. Everybody knew that it was one of a series of four; its name, and those of the others—*Orion*, *Monarch* and *Conqueror*—were pronounced with the deference due to sacred objects. The progress of this deadly counter in the world's power game was watched as though it, too, were part of the benefits of the exciting new century. The euphoria aroused by the Navy permeated fashions and songs. The Navy was the invincible arm of the supreme imperialist power, and for any other nation to attempt to match it was laughable impertinence. 'They may build their ships, my lads, and think they know the game, but they can't build the boys of the bulldog breed. . . .' Soon the *Thunderer*'s complement of 900, 'all British born', would be 'sailing every ocean, laughing foes to scorn'. Adulation of the Navy was not directly reflected in the crews' pay and conditions, but sailors were the nation's pets and— in the nicest possible way, of course—its sex-symbols, popularly imagined in immaculate white uniforms, romping boisterously through their service duties, peering through telescopes, openhandedly standing drinks in distant bars, being greeted by exotic girls in tropical ports, yet—essentially wholesome—returning innocent and unsoiled to faithful loved-ones at home. 'All the nice girls love a sailor. . . . He's the ladies' pride and joy !' Not only did he 'keep our foes at bay', but he represented civilized values—'You can trust a sailor, he's a white man all the while.' Mothers sang these songs while working about the house and bathing children; every concert, whether amateur or professional, had its flag-waving hornpipe-dancing number; the cinema pianist struck up 'a life on the ocean wave' when the White Ensign appeared on the screen. The indoctrination was unremitting. Those promenaders who were engaged in testing naval guns would give their families brief lectures on fire power while waving their walking-sticks in the direction of the long, low workshops of the Royal Ordnance factories where they spent their working lives.

They passed on from the Peak, walking between silver birches, making either for the bandstand in an area of pines, to listen to the regular Sunday evening concert, or simply to stroll along a road crossing the heath. The procedure was so regular that absentees from the promenade would be noticed and, if opportunity arose, inquiries made about them.

Essentially the parade belonged to the women, who insisted on going out because they had been 'tied to the house all the week'. The males stood back when their wives gathered round perambulators, and the freshly-ironed, lace-edged covers, which protected babies from the sun's glare as though they were the offspring of a master race in the tropics, were drawn back; but men were allowed to step forward and take the credit when their amiable, lovingly groomed dogs were admired.

The parade kept the women up to date on personal relationships, providing material for conversations, mostly spiteful, throughout the following week. Although the Estate was so new, the residents already formed an endogamous group, suspicious of intruders who, it seemed from the company they were keeping, might marry into it or take a member out of it. A young couple who walked about for an hour or so together were assessed as though they were irrevocably tied for life. Theoretically boys and girls were free to marry anybody they pleased; in practice they were not supposed to look around. On no more evidence than that of a few public conversations or an occasional Sunday stroll, girls were labelled as 'fast' or as flirts. The apparent break-up of a slight acquaintanceship was enough to start a rumour that a girl had been jilted. The effect was, of course, to load boy-and-girl friendships with a significance that produced a chilling wariness in both parties.

Of scarcely less interest to the promenaders was the pairing off of boys with boys and girls with girls. These relationships were safer, nicer and (the term was still being used a couple of decades later) healthier. What was meant, of course, was that no illegitimate births could result; any relationship was preferred to one which risked that disgrace. Boys and girls, and come to that, young men and women, were encouraged to have friends of their own sex. Provided these were well-dressed, well-mannered and not extravagant in their habits, they were welcomed, and were expected by parents to remain faithful. Frequent switches of friends incurred a social opprobrium only a few gradations less than that accorded to flirts and jilts. Whether adults were as unaware of the existence of homosexuality as they appeared to be I do not know; they must have heard of the Wilde case and presumably they attached some meaning to Sunday newspaper headlines of the 'Scoutmaster on Grave Charge' type. Whatever they knew or suspected, their minds were more at rest when they knew that their offspring were out with members of their own sex.

The women remain in the memory more than the men, not only because they ran the home but because they set the pattern of social life (such as it was) and were altogether more bossy, prejudiced, self-opinionated and elaborately turned-out.

Mrs Perry approaches, preceded by two small girls arm in arm and carrying prayerbooks in their white-gloved hands. One of the children is her daughter, Molly; fair-haired, blue-eyed, frail in build, Molly gives the impression of living on the verge of hysteria, and she is addicted to intensely emotional friendships. Her mother is tall, by Estate standards, and gaunt, with wary eyes, a thin nose, a turned-down mouth, and a jutting chin; from a distance she looks as though she is scolding her companion—the other girl's mother—but she is merely relating some occurrence which has outraged her and she intersperses her narrative with: 'I think it's a diabolical shame!' The word diabolical is not lightly used. The devil and all his works, the pomps and vanity of this wicked world, and all the sinful lusts of the flesh parade before her wherever she is. She goes to church twice on Sundays, she attends the vicar's Bible class, she is one of that band of women who busy themselves with flower vases in the church and parish hall, but her wrath, which she equates with the wrath of God, is never assuaged. Later I came to wonder what she was doing in the Church of England at all; her spiritual home was in a tin chapel among hell-fire preachers and moaning penitents. Behind walk the two husbands, followed by the small Perry boy who is jerked from side to side by a smooth-haired black dog as it takes unpredictable lunges at the end of the lead he is holding.

The Wyatt family, who have two thin, anxiously polite small sons, are Roman Catholics. I am very conscious of their religion, because the boys are permitted to leave the school classroom during Scripture lessons, the elder boy tells me about confession, and my mother, for reasons she never wants to discuss, fears Catholic priests; none the less, she and Mrs Wyatt are close friends and enjoy tea and biscuits together. Mr Wyatt is rather a mystery; unlike other local men, he has soft hands, he goes to an office, his sons seem in awe of him and he never shares their games, but his wife refers to him as Jim in their children's presence.

Of the Guest family I recall Mrs Guest, her daughter and the three sons, but the father is a vaguely nautical figure who, before settling on the Estate, worked as a ship's engineer and who was once known to utter a swear word. (The men never swore in their families' hearing and Mr Guest's lapse must have been a notable event. It was occasioned when a hailstorm blocked the outside drains and the ground floor of his house was flooded. 'I'm afraid my hubby said a bad word when he saw the damage,' Mrs Guest reported.) Feminine costume of the day allowed the wearer to walk without disturbing the external shape; the novelists' cliché of ladies sailing across the floor or along the street was an apt one. Mrs Guest moved majestically; she might have been standing on a moving platform. It was impossible to imagine that she would ever run. She entered a shop at the same controlled speed as she progressed up the church aisle. When she came to call her gestures, as she peeled off her gloves and raised her veil before sipping a cup of tea, seemed an almost startling act of exposure. Her most casual remarks carried a tone of calm authority.

Few other women attained quite such an impressive presence, but some approached it. Mrs Empson, tall and slim, accompanied by her ladylike daughter, was polite but reserved; as the wife of a regimental sergeant major, she was disciplined to a position of solitary dignity, a plane of existence midway between the officers and the non-commissioned officers. The family had moved to the Estate preliminary to the R.S.M.'s retirement. He did not attend these Sunday parades, perhaps because the disorderliness would have distressed him.

In contrast to this military family (who, it hardly needs saying, were 'not Labour' and were regarded by their neighbours as nice but unenlightened) were the Baxters. I do not remember Mr Baxter at all because his wife attracted so much attention by wearing neither hat nor gloves (even small girls were hatted and gloved when out for a formal walk) and by striding along revealing, at it were, the mechanism of walking. She seldom wore a coat or jacket but was usually seen with a shawl casually round her shoulders. This outfit marked her as a liberated woman, and she proclaimed herself a suffragette. Sex equality was axiomatic in the creed (as distinct from the practice) of progressive Estate dwellers, but suffragettes did not enjoy unqualified approval; the militants among them, by disturbing meetings, fighting policemen, damaging property and going to prison, were trying to shock bourgeois sensibilities, and in succeeding they were shocking the respectable working class too. Mrs Charlotte Despard was, because of her dignity, more respected than were the Pankhursts. People who had to consider what everything cost could not condone the breaking of windows for whatever cause; those who had schooled themselves to ladylike behaviour were affronted by newspaper pictures of women being forcibly restrained by policemen; to be sent to prison was a disgrace—heroics, if they outraged respectability, were disapproved of. Mrs Baxter flouted the conventions merely by her dress and manner. Active in various causes, she displayed posters in her front window (though the street she lived in was so quiet that they would have been seen mostly by the postman, the dustmen, deliverymen and the residents opposite) and at meetings she asked the kind of questions which began: 'Doesn't the speaker think. . . ?' and which contained the answer in themselves. Later, however, events were to show that she was suppressing passions which insisted on finding their expression.

The Humbert family came from Yorkshire via Germany. A few years earlier Krupps had recruited British engineering workers. After some years in Essen, Mr Humbert returned to England when his contract expired because he wanted his daughter and son to grow up in their own country. They were a quiet, introverted, solemn-looking family, who seemed to have brought with them the isolation they had felt in Germany. Hubert, an engineering apprentice, had acquired the polite formality of a young German and was regarded by other mothers as a model son. The self-effacing daughter, Dorothy, was also being steered towards a safe career; it was assumed, for no apparent reason, that she would not marry, and one day, if she could survive the fierce competition, she was to enter the Civil Service.

These I recall particularly clearly but there were many others. Two future mayors of the borough would pass, and so would such personalities as the barber (a sidesman at the Anglican church); the secretaries of local branches of the Amalgamated Society of Engineers and the Oddfellows; an alert, fox-terrier type of little Lancastrian named Higginson, well known as a committee chairman; another committee man named Fish and his schoolteacher son; the postmistress; the elementary school caretaker; the co-operative bakery roundsman (who had the dignity of a high-class coachman); a bearded, white-haired, courteous old man called Mr Chambers (who knew everybody because of his daily walks and the splendid monkey-puzzle tree in his front garden which passers-by stopped to admire); a cluster of Sunday school teachers carrying celluloid-covered prayer-books; the choir-mistress with her mother; and the postman (a retired soldier whose boots could be heard ringing on the pavements shortly after seven every morning).

All over Europe, from Düsseldorf's Königsallee to Malta's Kingsway, there would have been Sunday promenades, most of them much older-established than this one and many rather gayer. A band played in the woods, it is true, but there were no cafés or, indeed, anyone selling refreshments. None could surely have been more formal. Married women, unless related, never addressed each other by their Christian names. Neighbours who popped into each other's houses for cups of tea several times a week never advanced to the use of Christian or nicknames. So far as I was concerned Mrs Guest, Mrs Empson and Mrs Humbert had no first names. Men who worked together used first names in the workshop but in the presence of each other's families they reverted to formalities—possibly so that children should not learn to address their elders in a familiar manner. Fear of causing offence, of being deprived of dignity, governed forms of address in their social lives. Married women were conscious of their status; men of their position as wage-earners and householders. Mr Wyatt was the only man I knew whose Christian name was publicly mentioned by his wife.

Conversations, begun so formally, seldom departed from a routine of (in the ears of the waiting child) utter tedium. Children, less concerned about each other's *amour propre*, could express spontaneous thoughts among themselves, and could even give real answers to questions, but they soon learned that adult conversation was in the main an exchange of clichés. When the inevitable questions about their respective states of health were put, however, few people replied that they were very well, thank you. It was rare to hear anyone admit to being well. Everybody had what was known as a 'pet complaint'. 'It's that pain in my back.' 'I had one of my heads.' 'That knee's been playing me up again.' If not actually ill, they certainly suffered from various discomforts. False teeth fitted badly, spectacles were not properly prescribed, undiagnosed pains were endured for years out of a fear of being sent to hospital. Working hours were long—many of the men would have been putting in a sixty-hour week, and they were tired. But there was another reason why claims to ill health were so tenaciously maintained. Industrial workers had no paid holidays. If they wanted a holiday they had to ask for time off and lose money. The factory's demands were remorseless. Lives were lived to an unremitting timetable; years were spent in occupations which were actively disliked. The one way out for the men was the doctor's certificate, the industrial equivalent then of an Army leave pass. Waiting-rooms were crowded with men who, whatever their symptoms, were simply overstrained and dreadfully bored. It was useful to have a familiar complaint whose symptoms could be confidently related. The doctor behind the consulting-room door was to them less a healer—they did not expect or even want a cure but merely some amelioration of their condition— than a tribunal empowered to issue permits not to go to work. When he was seen to be writing out a certificate they could scarcely believe their good luck. Before them lay a whole week, and possibly even longer, of Sundays. The greatest joy was felt when a man already resigned to a renewal of the call by the alarm clock, the hurried breakfast, the scramble to get through the gates in time, the wishing away of the hours separating him from the evening and the journey home, presented himself at the surgery to be 'signed off', and the doctor said in an ordinary voice, as though unaware of the significance of that slip of paper: 'I think you'd better take another week.'

During sick leave freedom was not absolute. The patient, even though he could have leapt over hedges in his exultation, had to appear ill, as he was receiving sick pay from his union and friendly society, and the eyes of fellow-members would be on him. He could not work in his garden or leave his house after dark. If permitted to take a stroll as part of his recovery, he 'wrapped up well' and walked at a moderate pace. Solicitous neighbours, after inquiring about his condition, would remark: 'But I musn't keep you standing.' Probably the restrictions on activity were not unwelcome; few chances of doing nothing entered into their lives. Often the evenings during sick leave were pleasant. Branch treasurers—quiet, good-humoured men—called to deliver the few shillings of sick pay; they sat, drank a glass of stout and smoked a pipe, and related odd bits of news. Relatives and neighbours dropped in, offered their own diagnoses of the case, recited their own medical histories (everybody knew these by heart but nobody interrupted) and recommended such tonics as Wincarnis and Hall's Wine. Wives did not, of course, view their own illness as a period of liberation; for them to have to stay in bed meant domestic chaos; the symptoms they cultivated were such as could be used spasmodically to dominate the household when they felt like it and then just as suddenly thrown off—headaches, backaches, 'giddy turns' were their equivalent of the lightning strike.

So, for these few hours each week, an area of heath was taken over for this display of lower-class (but decidely not shabby) gentility. Occasionally the crowd walking in the roadway would part to permit the passage of a pony and trap or a small party of cyclists. The trap would be regarded admiringly; if smart, it was a status symbol and decorous enough to be exhibited on a Sunday. Cycling was only barely permissible. Many of the promenaders owned bicycles but they did not use them on Sundays; cyclists were an intrusion.

Eyebrows would have been raised, too, if the local poor had tried to usurp this promenade. Probably it did not occur to the poor to do so. They lived beyond the bounds of the Estate in a speculative builder's miscalculation, a Victorian terrace of large houses with high front steps and basements, where cloth-capped women in sacking aprons lounged round the entrances supported by their improvidently numerous children, and rag-and-bone men sorted through rubbish. At the local school these children, accurately and uncompromisingly known as 'the dirty kids' and feared as fighters and bullies, withdrew in the evenings and at the weekends to their ghetto. They constituted an unwelcome outpost of London poverty and a disagreeable reminder of the narrow gap which separated those confident-looking promenaders from utter poverty. So outlawed were they that they were not accorded membership of the working class; the title of 'worker' had been proudly appropriated by the house-owning, rose-growing Estate residents and to them it meant the people who really mattered.

As the families left the heath in the twilight and picked their way down the path from the Peak they grew silent. The weekend was over and tomorrow the men would assume a different role.

If explorers from another kind of society could have arrived on the Peak on a weekday morning and, alone and undisturbed as they would have been, had kept watch on the Estate, they might have concluded that an unseen power was giving orders from hour to hour. Chimneys started to smoke in unison; doors opened almost simultaneously and men emerged; an hour later children came out; then, on Mondays, hundreds of women hung white sheets on clothes lines to dry at about the same time. The observers would not know that each woman had worked with concentrated anguish so as not to be behind the others, and that anyone who was late felt it incumbent on her to offer an explanation (usually that the copper fire would not burn) to the housewives in neighbouring gardens. It was an active scene and—if the observers learnt to read the signs—a prosperous one. The sheets were all sound and as white as in any soap-powder advertisement. Filled out by the wind they were a festive sight, like a regatta. Worn or yellowing sheets were discarded; women held them up to the light, tugged at them and murmured: 'I can't hang that out any more.' In a way the Estate typified individualism; from the viewpoint of a collectivist it was deplorable that water was being separately heated in all those different sculleries, that each woman was performing identical operations, and yet the discipline was almost perfect. Without a single rule, without a planning department, managers or overseers, the system, if it can be called that, worked.

So quiet were the streets once the men and children were away that housewives' ears detected and identified every footfall, every movement of a horse and cart. The bakery roundsman found them at their doors, waiting to take in the warm white loaves. When the milkman came on his second delivery they were already at their doors with jugs. Yet they were deaf to periodic explosions which rattled windows and doors and caused cups to swing on dresser hooks. This was the sound of the local product being tested, and it no more disturbed them than the smell of the chocolate factory disturbs the inhabitants of Bournville.

The walled forbidden city where the product was made aroused very little curiosity, even though it was the source of the district's livelihood. The houses had been built, families were being reared, on the money earned there. Only its servants were allowed to pass its gates, through which could be glimpsed a couple of ancient cannon, a roadway and trees. Those who entered saw only their own area. Inside were degrees of accessibility, sections where outer clothes had to be changed, where matches, shreds of tobacco, any kind of dust were forbidden, and the roofs were constructed to fly off easily and thus not to contain an explosion. The wall dividing it from the town had been built generations before by convicts. Men who spent their working lives behind it declared that it exuded misery, that the prisoners' despair had been mixed into the mortar. No one's spirits, they declared, could be unaffected by it. The cheerful cycling party, still with countryside scents in their nostrils, uplifted by their spell of freedom, would cease to call to one another when, nearly home, they found themselves riding alongside that soot-blackened wall.

On a working day, viewed overall from the Peak, the Ordnance factories vibrated and erupted; smoke drifted across, veiling them in a perpetual haze; jets of steam spouted as in a volcanic landscape; an occasional flame flared and died; a muted rumbling and clanking rose and fell with the breeze. The woods behind the Peak had the shade, the coolness and the lofty spaciousness of a church; their sounds were of rustling leaves, murmuring birds and popping gorse bushes. The scene was utterly tranquil until a flash, as pervasive as lightning, preceded a sharp crack, which was followed by a deep rumbling wandering in a leisurely fashion round the woods, its reverbrations finally filtering out over the fields and orchards of Kent. A few birds, as though making a purely routine complaint, took off for a brief circuit and settled down again. Sand hung in the air over the butts where the projectile had landed. The peace of the woods seemed intensified, while the industry of death and destruction clattered on, producing cartridges, grenades, shells and guns, all made with the same precision as the finest scientific instruments.

The products were a threat to tear human flesh, to destroy buildings, to sink ships, to create a dead landscape of mud, water-logged pits and rusting metal out of woods and fields. When not being actively employed for these purposes they were paraded around the world, carefully tended, or stored in depots, as a warning that massive destruction could be organized at short notice. Yet the highly skilled and intelligent workers who produced all these devices scarcely thought beyond the product itself. They had the pride of armourers and the innocence of watchmakers. If some super-tribunal, anticipating Nuremberg, had called upon them to justify their life's work, had calculated how many people they had assisted in killing, what would they have said through their defence counsel? That the use to which armaments were put was not their business but the state's. That they were only one link in a chain which started with coal-miners and steel-workers and ended with soldiers and sailors. That they believed these weapons to be necessary to defend their country. That they were convinced that their country never had been and never could be aggressive, and that armaments were merely to preserve peace. Their counsel would certainly have argued in this way before the super-tribunal which would decide, as the Nuremberg tribunal was to do four decades later, that the accused were too low in status to be charged with complicity in crimes against humanity and, anyway, were so numerous that charging them would be an administrative impossibility and the exacting of any penalty a social disaster. But most of the men and their wives, however politically

alert they thought themselves, would have given a simpler and—
to them—unanswerable retort. They would have said of the Arsenal
that 'it makes work'. As they viewed that huge series of factories in
those pre-1914 days, they would have been very conscious that to
them it was the source of life. If those periodic explosions had ceased,
the community's heart would have stopped. Only a few years before,
men had become unemployed in the slump following the Boer War,
and had had to find work out of their trade (a humiliation equivalent
to what a barrister might experience if required to work as a
laundry-hand), to leave the district and even to emigrate. The mere
transfer of a department and its workforce to Scotland was bitterly
resented. Meetings protested against any threat of unemployment
and delegations to Whitehall urged their right to do whatever work
was going.

This argument was based on a concept of their rights which was
so fundamental that it needed no justification. 'I have a perfect right
to . . .' people would assert with such moral fervour that their title
to that particular privilege was seldom challenged. Speakers pandered
to this attitude with such phrases as 'the right to work' and 'the
right to earn a living'. That they, as a group, were demanding a near-
monopoly of the right to make instruments of destruction was
irrelevant; what superseded every other consideration was that they
should be paid for doing what they knew how to do. They were at
one with the silversmiths who for two hours cried: 'Great is Diana
of the Ephesians.'

On weekday nights, especially Saturdays, the lights of London
could be seen from the Peak. Clocks remained at Greenwich time all
the year, so even small children could be taken to look at the
spectacle without greatly postponing their bedtime. Late into the
night the London sky glowed as it has never done since. The *Strand
Magazine* had taught me what was going on there: in the West
End blazing theatres and restaurants, swells and flower girls, hansoms still competing with taxis; beyond that enchanted area a
different setting but no less gaiety in music halls and gaudy pubs,
street markets with naptha flares, shopkeepers shouting to clear their
stock. We could hear nothing of all this, and could only see the
golden reflection of thousands of lights on the clouds. It was
exhilarating but I was already being conditioned to perceive the
shadows between the lights. The conditioning did not arise from
political indoctrination or class envy; it did not arouse bitter emo-

tions but rather sadness, that melancholy underlying the Victorian songs which were still popular. Most children who took piano lessons learnt 'Won't you buy my pretty flowers?' with its mournful text: 'Underneath the gaslight's glitter, Stands a little fragile girl, Heedless of the night winds bitter, As they round about her whirl. . . . There are many, sad and weary, In this pleasant world of ours, Crying every night so dreary, Won't you buy my pretty flowers?' My mother could not see the lights without speculating, in an awed voice, about the horrors which lay between those illuminations and us. In that area, I learnt, in the Borough, Lambeth, Bermondsey and Deptford, the later the hour the poorer were the customers. The wives of the men in regular work had shopped on Saturday afternoon or in the early evening; from then on the customers' buying power diminished and the poor emerged to haggle for the fish, fruit and vegetables which would not last over until Monday, to grab the trimmings from joints and steaks, to relieve the bakers of their stale bread and cakes at a small fraction of the prices paid by those who had gone off with the fresher goods, dealing with the hoarse costers and yawning shopmen in terms of pennies, halfpennies and even farthings.

Immediately below were the gas lamps marking out the streets of the Estate, and the subdued lights from the windows. We stumbled home down the sandy path. The rows of houses looked unexciting but cosy and safe. As we entered our house my mother invariably said: 'Oh, isn't it nice to be home!'

3

The Unlovely Ladies

For most women, emancipation meant getting married and not having to go out to work. Far from being resentful at their relegation to the home all day, they regarded their exemption from wage-earning as the summit of feminine achievement. Already a quarter of the national labour force was female, but wage-earning women were—outside domestic service—a much more familiar sight in the North than in the South. Somehow these women on the Estate had also freed themselves from the burden of large families. Three children were about the acceptable maximum; any number over that would be contemptuously termed 'a horde of screaming kids' and the parents criticized as improvident. Overcrowding was no problem in this area of one-family houses. In fact, families had an amount of room which could well arouse the envy of flat-dwellers in the latter half of the century—three bedrooms, two downstairs rooms, a kitchen, a lot of cupboard space and an attic. No doubt Harold Nicolson, who when a Labour candidate suffered the distasteful experience of actually having to visit one of his loyal supporters in a 'horrid little house', would have found the dwellings on this bright new estate only marginally less horrid; certainly, compared with Knole or even Sissinghurst, they would have seemed rather cramped, but their occupants were very proud of them and willingly 'slaved' (a much-used word) to 'keep them nice'.

Housewives' hands, which felt like concrete, were evidence of the hard work entailed in clothes-washing, floor-scrubbing, grate-blacking, doorstep-whitening, brass-polishing, sweeping and dusting. None of the houses had electricity; domestic vacuum-cleaners and refrigerators had not been introduced. In the summer milk was boiled as soon as delivered and, in a vain attempt to stop it melting, butter was fetched from the shop in a glass dish which then stood in water on a shady window-ledge. Flies circled unceasingly round the hanging gas lamps, moved tirelessly up and down window panes, penetrated the larder despite the perforated zinc shield covering the window space, drowned themselves in jugs of milk and cups of tea, spotted mirrors, and died noisily on the flypapers which (apart from rolled newspapers) were the only available weapon against them. Exasperated by their buzzing and what she called their 'persistence', my mother would savagely break up their formations with a whirling duster; they scattered and resumed their circling as soon as she stopped. The only household aids were a large mangle with wooden rollers, a hand or treadle-operated sewing machine, a mincer, a gas fire (distrusted as giving off fumes), and—in the latest houses—a gas water-heater. That rush to get the sheets on the clothes-line alone entailed some exhausting effort, and then came blankets, the heavy clothing of the time, and the husband's working overalls.

Advertisements claimed that washday drudgery had been abolished, and a familiar picture showed a trim, unruffled housewife sitting beside a zinc bath, which stood on a table, reading a book while the clothes washed themselves. The young woman reading the book was merely the latest character in a long line of ad-men's housewives, such as Mrs Thrifty, the ardent user of a product called Harper Twelvetrees Glycerine Soap Powder in the 1860s (when Henry Mayhew noted the advertisement), who assured her friend Mrs Scrubwell that 'I scarcely ever rub our clothes now, and you know how black my Jim's shirts get at the Foundry.' Thanks to the pre-soaking, Mrs Thrifty's washing was, of course, on the line while Mrs Scrubwell was still 'up to the elbows' in suds, and Mrs Thrifty could not refrain from calling attention to her hands—'I don't stand rubbing the clothes to pieces and rubbing the skin off my hands at the washtub. . . .' Half a century later the Mrs Scrubwells, who had no faith in such magic, were still taking the skin off their hands.

Although the women did not bake bread, as did their northern contemporaries, a lot of their time was taken up preparing food. It was a matter of pride to have 'a meal on the table when they come in'. To that extent their days were tied to their husband's and children's timetable. Cakes, jams, and often pickles too, were prepared at home; it was considered slatternly to buy them. 'Shop cakes' and 'shop jam' were regarded with suspicion—'you don't know what's in them'. The more old-fashioned still retained a wariness about canned goods, referred to as 'tinned stuff', but canned sardines, salmon, pineapple and apricots (popular with children at teatime) were accepted.

The well-off (that is, those whose husbands earned as much as £2 a week—in golden sovereigns) had plenty to cook, and had no need—to use their own expression—to 'scrape'. The Sunday joint of English

beef or lamb (my mother would, for a family of three, specify that
it should be about 4½ lb) was considered a basic necessity. It reappeared in various guises during the week, but it was not eked out
parsimoniously. The rule, frequently affirmed in conversations, was
never to economize on food. The children of this class were, if anything, overfed. If a child did not habitually consume meals which
would have satisfied a healthy adult, the anxious mother consulted
the doctor. The contrasts in the local child population were marked;
even within this small area Two Nations existed, in a context not
envisaged by Disraeli. My first insight into the reality of poverty
came when a poor boy shyly explained, in answer to a concerned
teacher's questioning, that he had no breakfast and that at noon,
before going home, he collected money from his father—an hourly-
paid navvy working on a local road—so that his mother could
then buy food for a midday meal. The family lived from meal to
meal, and had no money left over to start the day.

Despite their frequent assertions that all they did was work their
fingers to the bone, women seemed to get pleasure out of housework.
My mother set about it with gusto and sang while she cleaned and
cooked—songs from *The Geisha Girl*, Kipling's 'Absent-Minded
Beggar' and another Boer War number beginning 'Three Good
Cheers for Buller, Powell and White', and the song commemorating
Grace Darling's rescue of sailors. She sang temperance songs learned
as a girl at the Band of Hope, such as 'Take away the wine glass,
Take away the beer, Water, bring me water, Water fresh and clear',
and 'Strike while the iron's hot, Strike one and all, Help drive from
out the field King Alcohol'. She sang with a mock seriousness,
dramatically emphasizing phrases so as to make them sound absurd,
or she imitated the accents of the Band of Hope leaders, whom she
described as rough, uneducated people although very sincere. In the
Berkshire village where she spent her childhood the Band of Hope
provided her only evening out; the organization attracted many
thousands of children of her generation. She had, as a member,
'signed the pledge' never to touch alcohol. When I realized the
solemn implications of this I was appalled. Her favourite remedy for
colds, which she prescribed for me even in my pre-school years, was
whisky in hot milk, and she often cheered me up with a mid-morn-
ing glass of port and a dry biscuit. Our household was never without
whisky, brandy, port, sherry, and crates of stout and India Pale Ale;
a stock of drink adequate to any demands of hospitality belonged

to my parents' concept of good housekeeping. They themselves were never even slightly drunk; none the less, I feared that my mother had committed a sin in not adhering to her pledge of total abstinence; one of the first lessons I absorbed was that God watches us every moment of our lives and that we are accountable for our slightest actions. She dismissed my fears for her soul by remarking, with a laugh, that she could not have joined the Band of Hope without signing the pledge. Later I learnt, from overhearing adult conversations, that as children quite a few of our neighbours had light-heartedly given their signatures in similar circumstances. For the sake of an evening out and an annual outing they would have signed anything. Yet although they now affected to feel superior about the Band of Hope, they regarded drunkenness with horror. Time and again they recalled an incident which had actually happened on the Estate. The wife of a man who later became known nationally as a trade-union leader spent her housekeeping money on drink, bought a sewing machine on hire purchase and failed to keep up the payments. She fought a running battle along the length of her street with a man who came to repossess it and triumphantly returned home with the machine, leaving him to carry off the empty cover. That she had bought an article on credit showed the degradation which drink could bring; everybody was sure that her husband, an upright man, could have had no knowledge of this transaction.

The struggle had been an unusually rewarding spectacle for the housewives who happened to be observing the street from behind their lace curtains. Their most absorbing occupation, when not otherwise engaged, was watching each other. Any woman entering a street during an afternoon, when the housewives had time to sit down, was gazed at with the intensity which coastal watchers would have applied in observing a foreign battleship steaming up the English Channel. According to the convention, women pretended to be unaware of this surveillance but, of course, they had prepared themselves with the care of actresses about to step from the wings. Going out to the local shops was not, therefore, a matter of a few minutes. Having got themselves into a condition to face scrutiny, they felt disinclined to return home quickly and dismantle the get-up, so they made the occasion last. Gossiping from front doorsteps was thought common, but it incurred no stigma when the parties were presentably dressed and out in the street. Small groups would stand in front of shops for an hour or more engaged in highly repetitive conversations, and once inside a shop they were difficult to shift, many of them seeming to have given no consideration to what they wanted to buy until actually confronted by the assistant.

Photographs show them in elaborate hats which have taken a long time to put on and in ankle-length costumes which, from their appearance, could be made of armour. Possibly the wary, distrustful expressions are more forbidding than they might be as the result of having to keep still while the photographer made the exposure, yet they evoke the personality of those young women. They look like frontiersmen's wives who half-expect that an arrow will suddenly affix itself in the log-cabin door behind them; and they were, in effect, pioneer settlers pushing forward the frontiers of a class. It is impossible to imagine them as 'girlies', those provocative, roguish, winsome, wide-eyed madcaps who, with saucy curls under saucy hats, were supposed to romp their way through the period, causing havoc among the 'knuts' and scandalizing the elderly. Nor were they remotely like those pensive, yearning, wasp-waisted ladies who, as pictured on the title pages of drawing-room ballads, were much given to sitting at the keyboards of grand pianos, gazing out of casement windows, drooping beside fountains, turning away after partings at garden gates, and smelling roses. They had reached womanhood by a different channel, and the small girls of the era could be observed following on the same track as they gossiped in groups and occasionally looked round to reprove some smaller child in the vicinity, strode purposefully on their shopping errands, kept a sharp eye on the scales and did not move from the counter until they had counted their change. Hawkers and gypsies must have known that feminine expression: that cautious stare at an outside world populated by rogues, the cold eyes which cast a disparaging glance at clothes-pegs, woven mats and baskets, the mouth pursed ready to say 'No, thank you!' in a tone which rejected further conversation, and a hand poised to shut the door smartly.

What were they aiming at in this meticulous concern for their appearance, in all that fussing over hats, gloves and scarves, in the careful brushing of costumes? It seems unlikely that they were, even in the broadest sense of the word, trying to be attractive. If they were cultivating sex appeal, it is not apparent to modern eyes. Make-up was unknown, and none of them had ever been to a hairdresser; indeed, no women's hairdressers existed for their class. They were acting the role of ladies, and they were offended if not referred to as such. Children were corrected if they referred to an adult female as a woman. In their eyes, to be a lady was to be free of human weaknesses, to embody respectability and dignity, to occupy an invulnerable position in the community. 'Nobody can point a finger at me . . .' they would say. But whatever admirable qualities they sought to acquire, they did not achieve grace and charm; their characteristic manner was a defensive irritability.

Fears big and small beset them. Even before the shutter is released the women in the family albums know that the picture is not going to come out well, that the money is being wasted and would have been better spent on a new sun-blind or a pair of gloves. They rarely smile in the pictures, but if they do it is a deferential smile, as if they are asking a favour which every sensible person knows cannot be granted. Already they can hear themselves saying: 'Don't I look silly?' as the prints are handed round. They are aware of their presumption. 'Who do I think I am, having my photograph taken at my age?' Their mothers, husbands, sisters, children insisted that they wanted a picture; for themselves, they hate themselves in a photograph. Behind these thoughts while posing in the studio are others, ranging from dud half-crowns, short weight, and gloves splitting at the seams, to children's coughs, the security of their husbands' jobs, to that supreme dread, voiced in countless conversations and no doubt fearfully insured against in prayers.

Because of that fear of cancer, they tried to ignore twinges of pain, dismissing them as 'just a touch of' rheumatism, indigestion, anything plausible. 'I've had pains like this before and they always went away.' Other people were appealed to for support, to say: 'I've often felt like that. It doesn't mean anything.' Advertisements and encyclopaedias of home medicine were studied, patent medicines taken. Anxiety communicated itself to the entire household. News of acquaintances' afflictions, rapidly circulating, came as bad omens. 'The doctor's given her a letter to take to the Middlesex.' The neighbour concerned, referred to a hospital for a further diagnosis, was already written off. The trip to the hospital was an ordeal in itself. The journey to London was probably made on a workman's ticket; these were issued for trains which arrived at the London terminus not later than 8 a.m. Patients often waited in a huge room for several hours, moving along the wooden benches until they came to the front, then standing in the final queue moving up to the

[47]

specialist. By this time their fears were overshadowed by a longing to escape, to be back in the isolation of their homes. Probably at this stage they told the specialist only half the truth, not wanting to prompt him to keep them in. Subsequently, of course, the experience made dramatic conversational material. Some of their happiest and most relaxed hours were spent exchanging medical misinformation over tea and biscuits.

Children were warned that they were in constant risk of 'the fever'. 'Don't stand near that drain,' passing adults would say to children. The fear dated from a not far distant time when open sewers ran through towns and villages and the death of infants was a commonplace occurrence. The drains in the street gutters on the Estate carried away nothing more noxious than rainwater, yet they were suspected of spreading a fearsome miasma. Another dread—and a justifiable one—was caused by the proximity of the 'dirty kids', for whom the promising new century had brought nothing except, perhaps, the compulsory shaving of their heads when they had ringworm, periodic inspections of their hair for lice and the occasional delousing of their clothes. Another matter on which Estate parents felt strongly was the risk their children ran of hearing slum language; children, as they frequently remarked, always follow the worst example, so they had to be protected from acquiring a 'common' accent and from committing the sin of blasphemy.

Running through their thinking and conversation was the belief in retribution, and they imbued their children with it. Hovering uncomfortably close—I imagined him as suspended above an orchard near our house—was a supernormal overseer, who allotted awards and, much more frequently, punishments. 'I don't know what I've done to deserve that,' they would say, and they would review their recent behaviour to discover how they had incurred chastisement. Pagan and Christian beliefs mingled; every kind of superstition was observed. Spilling salt, walking under ladders, seeing the new moon through glass, wearing green, encountering one magpie but not two, bringing may blossom into the house, breaking a looking-glass, a picture falling from the wall, opening an umbrella in the house, laying shoes (even a new pair just purchased) on a table, putting the left shoe on first—all could precede misfortunes ranging from a saucepan of milk boiling over to a death in the family. Scoffers were silenced by evidence: when a picture crashed down in my grandmother's house she said: 'Somebody's going', and her apparently healthy husband died within a week. Like the hosts of Midian, malevolent forces prowled and prowled around.

Perhaps some of these superstitions have proved more tenacious than Christian beliefs, but at that time religion was a power influencing almost every household; along with the British Empire, the church was still enjoying its heyday.

4

The Goodness and the Grace

Anglicans were the most numerous of the local Christians, the most prosperous, and probably the most formal. They did not enter the church except after a prolonged preparatory period of face-washing, hair-combing, nail-cleaning and the careful consideration of clothes; one expression used for a garment showing signs of ageing was: 'I can't wear that to church any more.' There was none of that Latin familiarity with the church, no popping in at odd times to light a candle, pray or sit in a reverie. Unlike the Primitive Methodist chapel, the church could not be hired for meetings or lectures. It belonged to Sunday, along with the roast joint, the scent of lavender and mothballs, the clean, scratchy underwear, the immaculate gloves, and the coin kept handy for the collection (children gave a half-penny or a penny and so did some adults; the maximum contribution was sixpence).

On Sundays the vicar could count on having the church comfortably full in the mornings, and so packed in the evenings that sometimes extra chairs had to be carried in from the Parish Hall. The church's notice board bore no eye-catching slogans; the young were not tempted with ping-pong, coffee and dancing. The vicar did not dress to look like one of the chaps; he and his clerical suits (black or white according to the season) and collar were inseparable; he regarded himself, and he was regarded, as a man apart—anyone who saw his manner of proceeding through the streets could have no doubt of that. People were both gratified and embarrassed to be greeted by him; conversation during these encounters was punctuated by unnaturally loud bursts of laughter. Royal persons moving among the populace seem to produce the same effect.

He and his church worker, Miss Carey, were punctilious in visiting parishioners. She, recognizable at a distance by her white hat and gloves, distributed the parish magazine and made genteel conversation over tea; in contrast to the jolly vicar she moved in and out of houses in the manner of someone who has arrived late at church and is anxious not to disturb the service. I was too young to know whether their visits brought comfort to the sick and the distressed.

I was conscious only of the flutter caused by the arrival of one or the other, the hasty production of a clean tablecloth, the appearance of the thin china, and the general conviction that they were so refined, so remote from the rough and tumble of everyday life, that they would be pained by hearing even a mildly vulgar word. 'I don't know what the vicar would think if he heard you say that !' was a formula which greeted a very remotely risqué remark. The neighbourhood was mostly occupied by young families, who were at a time of life when they were least in need of sympathy. In that excessively reticent age the sort of problems now referred to psychiatrists would not have been mentioned to anybody, not even a family doctor. The church representatives would have seen parishioners only on their best behaviour, pure in word and deed, and the parishioners would have regarded the visits as setting the seal on their respectability.

The vicar's sermons were equally undisturbing. Despite his loud voice and the church's bathroom echo, he was never tempted to conjure up terrifying visions of a flaming pit. Yet, when intoning not his own words but those of the liturgy, he was something more than an amiable middle-aged gentleman. Church services were not merely a social occasion. The ceremony generated its own power; during the psalms, led by the disciplined choir at a cracking pace, force flowed through the congregation. Perhaps Mr Charlesworth's sermons were so placid because he felt that there was little more for him to say, that the church's message had already been received. It was the church's calendar which marked the seasons and infused them with its emotions. The New Year was another year of our Lord. Lent was variously observed, or by some not observed at all, but nobody could be unaware of what period it was. Good Friday was not just a Bank Holiday; it was a day of mourning; the atmosphere in the streets was subdued. I recall the elation as we sang 'Jesus Christ is risen today' and the cheerfulness of the after-church promenaders. We were not celebrating an event which had occurred in the remote past but one which had been announced that morning. Imbued as it was with the spirit of husbandry, the congregation sang with special heartiness: 'All is safely gathered in, Ere the winter storms begin.' For me that hymn evoked all the cosiness of the change of season, when for the first time the heavy curtains were drawn, the open fire lit and the toasting fork taken from its hook. Christmas was a time of mystery and wonder.

Sunday was for the observance of the Christian religion. Everybody, by dressing for it, recognized that it was no ordinary day. Even those consciously enlightened mechanics who had absorbed the self-confident rationalism of the late Victorian era, who had read Darwin and Wynwood Reade, who were convinced that there was no cosmic secret which men who could build steam engines would not ultimately unravel, were outwardly conformist and anxious not to offend believers' susceptibilities. They did not, as on Saturdays, walk through the streets in old clothes carrying gardening tools. If seen on their plots on Sundays they were in their best suits, leading similarly attired acquaintances round the beds, and pointing with their pipe-stems at plants of particular interest.

Conformity was a comparatively uncomplicated matter for these men; they were simply required to dress up and refrain from any activity which looked like work. That was only one aspect of seemly conduct on the Sabbath, however. The line between the proper and the improper could not be so easily defined. Walks were permissible, of course, but what about such fringe activities during the walks as playing ball with the children? Could the licence to walk be extended to cycling? Opinion generally was that it could not. Was it irreverent (or likely to shock neighbours) to play the piano, and if a liberal view were taken and piano playing allowed, ought the performance to be confined to what was called sacred music? Was sewing 'work', or was it free of sin provided you did not use the sewing machine?

Rulings on such delicate issues were usually delivered promptly and unequivocally by the woman of the household. Was there a sinister significance in the circumstance that more women than men went to church? To the armoury of splitting heads, aching backs, swollen feet and temper tantrums employed to maintain dominance over a family was added the heavy-calibre weapon of the religious sanction. Not a few of the housewife-members of the Bible class were at home law-givers and prophets. God was invoked on any day of the week to reinforce prohibitions of 'answering back', pouting, squabbling, entering the house with muddy boots, leaving toys scattered over the floor, appearing late for meals, leaving dirty finger-marks on doors, and going on shopping errands with a bad grace. Such simple misdemeanours were elevated to the level of manslaughter by the warning that they were bringing a mother to an early grave. Sensitive children's feelings were harrowed by the prediction: 'When you see me lying in my coffin you'll be sorry for the way you behaved.' The offending children were shortening their own life span by forgetting the Fifth Commandment: 'Honour thy father and thy mother; that thy days may be long in the land which the Lord thy God giveth thee.' Everlasting damnation could be incurred merely by the use of a taboo word. 'Fool' was banned because of Matthew iii, 22: 'Whosoever shall say, Thou fool, shall be in danger of hell fire.' The word 'hell', by the way, could be uttered only in a scriptural context; otherwise people said 'Hades' or 'down below'. A similar hazard attached to the word 'bald'; an innocent reference to baldness in the course of describing a man could lead to a sharp reminder of the familiar passage in Kings. 'Damn' caused gasps of horror.

Nobody could escape constant awareness of religious institutions, which had a way of taking over news stories and making them its own. Consider the wreck of *The Titanic* in April 1912. Faith in God was fostered by an event which might well have dispelled it. The disaster made an impact which later generations accustomed to loss of life and material on a large scale can scarcely imagine. The shock was a double one: consternation at the number of lives lost and incredulity that such an accident could happen to a magnificent piece of engineering. Shipwrecks, apart from the kind of collision which sank the little *Princess Alice*, belonged in those pictures, still to be seen in many households, depicting fishermen's wives gazing hopelessly at the raging sea. Local craftsmen discussed the event as though they were personally hurt by this affront to men's skills, but the clergy seemed not to regard it as a set-back. The ship's orchestra had played 'Nearer my God to Thee' as the passengers crowded the rails on the slanting decks, and this hymn was fervently sung in the church and, less fervently, during morning assembly at the local school. Was there a touch of defiance in the choice of another hymn, 'Eternal Father, strong to save'? The opening strains of these hymns must still recall *The Titanic* to those who were children at the time. At the Wesleyan Hall (a half-hour's walk from the Estate) the occasion was dramatized, the hymns being sung by massed choirs to precede an interminable monologue by a female elocutionist, which started with the discussion of the plans to build a monster liner (she injected tremendous poignancy into the word 'unsinkable') and ended with the vessel's final plunge. Deeply impressed, the audience stood in silence, and were then led by the minister in the Lord's Prayer. God had come out of the whole affair very well.

Interwoven with these Sunday memories is a disturbing awareness of the existence of (as they appear in photographs) sepia-coloured children, skinny underclad little creatures, their hair uncut, their legs and feet bare as they stand awkwardly and unsmiling before the camera. They seem very close because we see their pictures so often, projected on a wavy white sheet by a magic lantern. All we know about them, apart from their colour, is the horrifying fact that they are heathen, and that is all we need to know. The warm pennies clutched inside our gloves, the mission boxes which stand on tables and coat-stands just inside the front doors of so many homes, the jumble sales—all this activity is to rescue them from their blindness in bowing down to wood and stone. A hymn tells us what their trouble is: 'The Bible they have never read, They know not that the Saviour said, Suffer little children to come unto me.' If they did not receive all the Bibles they needed it was not our fault. I was not a sceptic, the word heathen to me meant a state of existence horrible to contemplate, I did not doubt Mr Charlesworth's frequent assertions that we ought to consider ourselves particularly fortunate, no flicker of cynicism crossed my mind when we were reminded of Ann and Jane Taylor's verse: 'I thank the goodness and the grace, Which on my birth have smiled, And made me, in these Christian days, A happy English child.' Yet, willing believer though I was, I could not believe that those children in the lantern slides would ever read the Bible. Like most children then, I owned a Bible. From my fourth year, when my father—without fancy aids—taught me to read, I was addicted to print; if I was left without printed matter in my hands, my gaze wandered hungrily to the text on tins and packets; it took me no time to learn the knack of reading, when travelling, the upside-down print on a folded newspaper held by a passenger sitting opposite. Yet I found the Bible unreadable. It was not for lack of trying. Repeatedly a picture of a missionary handing out Bibles to grateful savages or of a lonely shepherd and a grandchild with their heads together over a Bible caused me to return to my Bible, determined to read it for hours until (as happened in stories) my heart was filled with joy. No joy resulted. The thin pages remained unturned. Yet we were constantly told of the great happiness which was ours if we were willing

to receive it. Did I merely imagine that a sense of anticipation preceded services? Or that, during the sermon, hope oozed away?

On one occasion the church seemed about to canalize the community's latent emotions. One of Mr Charlesworth's successors, a
man with a German-sounding name which was to be a nuisance to
him (ultra-patriots referred to him as 'the German parson'), somehow
got himself involved in promoting an organization called The King's
Messengers. Announcements from the pulpit and in the Sunday
school, paragraphs in the parish magazine, the distribution of leaf-
lets, constituted a heavy publicity build-up in an area where social
life was narrowly restricted. Membership cards were to be issued,
their holders to have a special role in the local life of the church.
What sparked off such a high degree of expectancy is a mystery.
Even people who attended church only at Christmas and Easter reminded each other of the inaugural meeting; children caught the
fever and calculated how they could finish their homework in time
to go. If participants had been promised initiation into hitherto most
closely guarded secret rites they could not have displayed more
fervour. Usually at evening meetings during the week a few people
drifted in rather late, tended to sit spread out at the back and were
implored to come forward to fill the front rows. The ladies' choir
(not to be confused with the church choir, which was exclusively
male), plagued by absenteeism, was up to strength and pressed for
space on the platform. When the audience had taken all the seats in
the body of the hall people were still arriving. Additional chairs
were fetched from the church by helpful men. Newcomers stood at
the sides and in the gangways. The doors could not be closed. Exhilaration mounted as more people crowded in and were greeted by
gloves and hymn books waved by those already seated. Sensing that
some action was needed to bring the gathering to order, the choir-
mistress stood up, put on her pince-nez, picked up her baton and
sent her ladies into an opening hymn.

When the last verse was sung the vicar, who had witnessed none
of the proceedings out front, appeared. Unlike his predecessor, he
was not large, round-faced and jovially loud. He was slight, with a
thin, troubled face and short, bristly, grey hair. His voice did not
carry so well, and he was accustomed to look straight ahead as
though he were wearing blinkers; probably he was embarrassed by
having, as a public figure, to recognize people. As usual, he came in
through a door at the far end of the hall, his eyes on a few papers.

Instead of finding a clear passage to the platform, he had to squeeze past his eager parishioners. Apologies were murmured. A relief actor who had accepted what he thought was an engagement to walk through a part in a familiar repertory piece and found himself expected to play the lead in a gala performance might have had similar feelings. The overcrowded platform offered no foothold. He made his way round to the front and stood still, the ladies' choir behind him, his hopeful flock solidly jammed in this usually roomy pen, all tensely waiting to be led into a crusade. For several moments he stood, looking from side to side. This evening his blinkers were no protection. Perhaps he realized that, in such a situation, a preacher's words might send a congregation into rapturous chanting, cause them to fall down in worship of hallucinatory heavenly figures, find themselves miraculously cured of their physical ills, shout in strange tongues, laugh and weep and embrace each other. He spoke: 'I'm afraid I hadn't anticipated quite such a response this evening.' Another silence followed. It was unforgettable, poignant; imagine a much-advertised performer on the high wire, heralded by a drum roll, poised in the limelight, putting out one foot and then withdrawing it, unable to take a single step, stared at by the crowd as he hesitates; the sudden drop from exhilaration to apathy could not have been more painful. The moment for take-off had passed. He was, of course, very glad to see everybody, he said. His first duty was to . . . and with such comfortable clichés inhibiting inconvenient emotions, the vicar told his passive audience of the objects of The King's Messengers (even the most moderate church-goers could have drafted those for themselves), called on the choir to perform, produced the expected homiletic discourse, led prayers, and announced that members would be enrolled at the door. The next assembly of the Messengers was much less disturbing—a late start and plenty of space for everybody—and gradually they disbanded without having set the community aflame with religious zeal.

I cannot remember when I did not find Sunday school humiliating. Attendance was not, of course, compulsory; my parents did not insist that I should go; yet it never occurred to me to stay away. Sunday had me in its grip. Inconveniently soon after Sunday dinner, a meal which could have been indefinitely extended, after its courses were finished, with fruit, cakes and biscuits, I hurried to the Parish Hall, repeating passages from the Catechism or whatever had been set the previous week for learning by heart. Children learn easily

by heart and I could confidently gabble any verses after reading
them through a few times. I tried to attach a meaning to them. I
pondered over this: 'When I was a child I spake as a child, I understood as a child, I thought as a child: but when I became a man I
put away childish things. For now we see through a glass, darkly;
but then face to face.' Those words still evoke the odours of roast
mutton, mint sauce and baked potatoes, and a mental picture of a
man who, having put away childish things, is—for reasons which
will no doubt one day be revealed—peering through a piece of
smoked glass as though looking at a solar eclipse. Nobody ever provided a more credible picture. Now it seems inconceivable that,
heavy with food, I should have walked through the streets muttering
to myself: 'Or ever the silver cord be loosed, or the golden bowl
be broken, or the pitcher be broken at the fountain, or the wheel
broken at the cistern. Then shall the dust return to the earth as it
was: and the spirit shall return unto God who gave it.' These and
other passages jangled round my brain for years without slotting
themselves into any system of knowledge. The so-called 'Sunday
school teachers', many of them teenagers, had no more idea than I
had of what this language meant. I doubt the serious purpose of an
institution which permits theology to be taught, even in its early
stages, by the immature and the uninformed.

Religious teaching was degraded by the Sunday school just as the
local school's daily 'act of worship' was a parody of a religious
service. The morning assembly at school was a brisk affair, the
various classes marching in to the sound of martial music on the
piano, the teachers barking like drill sergeants at the pupils not to
shuffle, to pick their feet up, hold their heads back, swing their arms,
stick their chests out. 'Let us pray' was rapped out like a command.
The hymn was interrupted by a smart tap of the headmaster's baton
on his desk and a bellow to the effect that the school was sharp or
flat, singing at the wrong tempo or with insufficient enthusiasm. In
the circumstances, what appeared to be his favourite hymn—John
Keble's 'New every morning is the love Our wakening and uprising
prove'—tended to sound a cruel mockery, and, in the unlikely event
that any spark of spiritual inspiration had been kindled, it would
have been promptly extinguished by the next stage in the ritual,
when the headmaster, with occasional ferocious glances over the top
of the paper he was holding, read out a series of admonitory notices.
After this alarming performance the classes, stamping like little

guardsmen, were hounded to the comparative peace of their class-rooms, there—if they were lucky—to spend half an hour or so illus-trating Biblical scenes with coloured chalks on coarse brown paper and getting over the demonstration of Christianity's association with authority.

Once a year the Roman Catholic church asserted itself. The Sunday crowd, instead of promenading on the heath, lined the route of the Corpus Christi procession. The exotic glitter, colour and incense, the canopy above the priest, the column of nuns were less surprising to me than some of the worshippers in the long line of Catholics who followed. There, among the respectable and well-dressed, were rough lads who seemed to me improbable churchgoers. Scarcely recog-nizable with their hair slicked down, their sober suits and polished boots, they were singing not self-consciously but confidently, obviously at ease. Youths of that type never appeared at the Angli-can church or at the annual fête and gala; it was difficult to imagine them submitting to any discipline yet, I realized with awe, they confessed their sins and participated in the mystery of the Latin Mass. Emotionally I was drawn to Catholicism, but restrained by my mother's attitude from showing any interest in it. Unable to resist the spectacle of the procession, she stood behind me emanating hostile vibrations. After the procession had retreated behind the tall railings bordering the convent grounds, making its way along the gravel paths among the clipped laurels and religious statues, we resumed our customary walk across the heath. She spoke from a tight throat, as she did when angry. 'Those fat old priests!' She was silent as people passed, because she did not want to be overheard. 'Lace round their surplices! . . . They get people in their clutches!' Then came her most crushing judgement. 'They're bigoted.' This attitude never prevented her from having Catholic friends; she was uninterested in theology and had little, if any, idea of the doctrinal differences between Catholics and Anglicans. She seldom expressed strong feelings about issues which did not affect her immediately and personally, but on Corpus Christi something moved her to anger.

While the Anglican children were clustered round their teachers in the Parish Hall, and the harmonium was accompanying the sing-ing in the Primitive Methodist Chapel (which smelt overpoweringly of varnish and coconut matting), another meeting was proceeding in a large wooden hut which backed on to a builder's yard. When the hut windows were open, a pleasant and faintly exciting smell of newly-sawn timber, turpentine and creosote floated in. Originally this construction had been the site hut, a place for workmen to brew their tea and eat their sandwiches. Now, tidied up a bit, the interior decorated in institutional green, the signs Ladies and Gentlemen painted over two doors at the rear, and equipped with a small platform and a piano, it had been promoted to the status of a hall. It was commonly referred to as The Hall, and it was at that time the principal meeting place. On Sunday afternoons it housed a gathering of people unassociated with churches and chapels.

Had the participants declared themselves fundamentalists, theosophists, spiritualists or practitioners of black magic they would have been relatively easy to describe. They included, if you like, the cranks of the neighbourhood, a miscellaneous lot, some of whom had moved to the Estate out of a belief that it would become a kind of Bournville or Port Sunlight but without what they saw as capitalist paternalism. A few were, or tried to be, vegetarians, and these were prone to discuss to what extent they could, to be consistent, consume or wear animal products. Some were teetotallers, who were careful to distinguish themselves from chapel-goers by the added argument that publicans, brewers and tobacco manufacturers made private profits. Some were opposed to vaccination against smallpox (a live issue at the time) and vivisection. Others were just thoughtful working men. All would have regarded themselves as politically advanced. But, because of the fun which was poked at cranks, and the fears that Labour supporters were revolutionaries, it is necessary to qualify these descriptions. Not one wore sandals or a homespun cape. Free love would have shocked them. It is probably safe to say that none had read a word of Marx or Engels. When they went to meetings they wore their best clothes; in appearance they were conventionally petit bourgeois. In fact, they were torn between a desire for conventionality and a need to assert their enlightenment. Church attendance seemed to imply a belief that the world was created in six days and that animals marched two by two into the ark.

Yet, unable to answer the call of the church bell, they needed a form of Sunday observance. They felt impelled to meet in a reverent atmosphere, to sit in rows, to sing what they would probably have called secular hymns, to listen to solemn readings of good works, to hear discourses which were as packed with vague beneficent-sounding phrases as were Mr Charlesworth's sermons. What they were doing in this imitation church service is a question they do not seem to have asked themselves. God was not, so far as I can ascertain, mentioned, yet they seemed to be addressing someone or something. They condemned greed, self-seeking and oppression, and they believed in the perfectibility of man. Any passing Baptist might have slowed his pace on hearing voices raised in a familiar hymn, 'These things shall be !' The rendering began normally :

> These things shall be ! A loftier race
> Than e'er the world hath known shall rise,
> With flame of freedom in their souls,
> And light of knowledge in their eyes.

The second verse, about this race daring all that may plant man's lordship firm, on earth, and fire, and sea, and air, also ran as expected. But if the listener had waited he would have heard a verse which did not occur in John Addington Symonds's text :

> They shall be simple in their homes,
> And splendid in their public ways,
> Filling the mansions of the state,
> With music and with hymns of praise.

If the questions which this verse raises were asked, I did not hear them. Were they all in favour of domestic austerity and public grandeur? What sort of mansions of the state had they in mind? Who or what was to be praised? Was there perhaps something prophetically sinister about that verse? Since then we have seen mansions of the state crammed with jubilant citizens and have heard their hymns of praise, addressed not to some nebulous spirit but to the leader and the party.

On those tranquil Sunday afternoons they too observed the spirit of the day, not examining their beliefs critically, innocent of the realities of politics, and comforting each other by their unanimous faith in science, culture and self-improvement. If they were shy about acknowledging a deity, at least they had their saints. They could contemplate the rather odd features of Robert Owen, whose portrait hung on the wall and whose followers were commemorated in a local street name. Their own bookshelves and pictures, the lectures some of them chose to read when invited to do so, revealed a reverence for Ruskin, G. F. Watts and William Morris. They wanted religion without religion.

A writer should keep clear of ghosts if he wishes to retain his credibility, but no honest report of what people thought and talked about could omit ghosts. The subject occurred in conversations with some frequency. Few would admit to 'believing' in them but they none the less related anecdotes—in the jocularly defensive way that people discuss occult phenomena—of personal experiences featuring a ghost. Certain of the hauntings were of the dubious kind accompanied by natural happenings—storms, fogs, moonlight. Or the presence of discarnate entities was suspected in old houses where the timber creaks, wind moans along passages, and the plumbing gurgles. But there were others where the apparition appeared without theatrical props.

My father was the reluctant percipient in what psychical researchers would call a spontaneous case. He related it not jocularly but as though he had something discreditable to confide. Born in 1875, he had grown up in an era of rationalism. He gained an apprenticeship to engineering, an up-and-coming occupation when Britain was the workshop of the world and one which had its own philosophy (at least, he thought it did) of absolute integrity. An article either worked properly or it did not; there was no making do. His standards of precision applied to everything around him; doors had to swing properly, locks turn smoothly, door catches fasten firmly, drawers slide in and out without sticking, knives cut, w.c. cisterns flush at the gentlest pull, fires leap into flame on the application of a single match, timepieces neither lose nor gain, taps turn off without dripping. Carlyle was still read in those days, and craftsmen warmed to such sentiments as: 'The foul sluggard's comfort: "It will last my time." ' Man was master of his environment, and need put up with no annoyance from the objects he had created. Philosophical discussion affronted him; his reaction on hearing an explanation of Bishop Berkeley's theory resembled Dr Johnson's. I never heard him exclaim 'Rubbish!' with such scorn. Did all those material things which he so scrupulously sketched, measured, cut, filed, welded, polished, oiled and bolted together exist only in his mind? Had he studied trigonometry, mechanics, metallurgy in order to produce a mass of illusions? On religion he was non-committal. 'If there is a supreme power', he once remarked to a woman evangelist who he considered had pestered him too long, 'we know nothing about it and I doubt whether it is concerned with us as individuals.' He never accompanied my mother to church and I do not think she ever sought to persuade him to. He dealt in the tangible. The ghost he saw demanded a concession in his thinking which he was not prepared to make.

The experience occurred when he was a very young man and he and his parents were spending Sunday afternoon with his widowed grandmother who lived in a small farmhouse overlooking the River Medway. While the elders were chatting my father went out for some fresh air in the garden. He was sitting there when he saw his grandfather come out of the open back door, walk slowly down the garden path, pausing as a gardener does to inspect plants, then lean on a gate to look at the view. Suddenly the old man was not there. My father found it difficult to analyse his feelings. In the first moments, it seemed, he accepted the figure as his living grandfather. It was a sunny afternoon, his grandfather was dressed as he normally would have been, and he walked like a solid figure. When there came the realization that this must be a ghost, my father experienced no chill, felt no horror, but simply stared in fascination. He was staring when the figure disappeared. For some little time, he said, he sat wondering what to do, afraid that an announcement of what he had seen would be met by incredulity, scorn, or laughter. It might even distress his grandmother. Reluctantly he decided that he could not keep the incident to himself; he disliked having secrets on his mind. A lively conversation was going on in the parlour. The fact that he had to interrupt the talk increased his fear of an irritable response. Bluntly he exclaimed that he had just seen Granddad in the garden. Calmly his grandmother asked: 'What did he do?' When my father told her she said: 'Oh, yes. He often does that.' Other members of her family nodded. They too had, at various times, seen the apparition. The party then reverted to the previous conversation, as though nothing out of the way had happened.

He could not come to terms with this incident; its possible implications threatened to shatter his ideas of the rational. He sought to explain it away by giving it a name, a trick adopted by much more practised thinkers than he was. Having decided that ghosts cannot be, people have to find another word for what they see. He would have liked to say that it really did not happen, that he had fallen asleep and had an unusually realistic dream. But he was certain that

[62]

he was awake; anyway, he was not of an age to doze off. It must, he declared, have been a hallucination. Considering his abrupt dismissal of Bishop Berkeley he was on dangerous ground here. What about the other people who had seen the old man go through the identical ritual? He conceded that their experience confirmed his claim that he could not have been asleep. They had simply had a hallucination too. I tried to argue that something—we did not need to call it a ghost if he disliked the word—had happened on various occasions. He was willing to affirm the apparent reality of his experience; his grandfather had looked as real as I did at that moment. The other family members who had seen the old man were certainly telling the truth; they could not have brought themselves to concoct a story, even if they had had a motive for doing so, and he was sure that he had never, before going into the garden on that afternoon, heard that the place was haunted.

His farming relatives could calmly accept the evidence of their eyes. As a member of a later generation he felt bound to believe that, as ghosts do not exist, it follows that you cannot see them.

I do not recall that the local clergy, teachers, police or anybody else ever took credit for the fact that crime on the Estate was non-existent. The local newspaper printed columns every week of police court proceedings against pickpockets, shoplifters, Saturday-night brawlers, the drunk and incapable, vagrants who 'failed to live an honest and industrious life', debtors, men who defaulted on maintenance orders, women who concealed a birth; but all these offences were committed in those grey, smoke-ridden areas of south-east London which the eye did not dwell on while enjoying the distant glory of St Paul's against the sunset sky. The offenders, in the court reporters' clipped style, were accorded no human dignity. Once their full names, without prefix, were given, and their addresses (when they had anywhere to live) set out in full so that there could be no ambiguity about their identity, there came the sad description: 'of no occupation', 'a labouring man', 'describing herself as a house-wife', 'said by the prosecution to be the mother of eight children', 'unable to give an account of himself'.

My mother who, like all her acquaintances, eagerly studied the local paper although always referring to it disparagingly, was horri-fied by the frequently appearing phrase 'of no fixed abode'. She would speculate on how anyone could live without a regular bed to sleep in. She was haunted by the story of one vagrant who slept under a truck. Stormy nights, snow, heavy frosts, reminded her of him. Her imagination pictured him in a railway siding, with nothing but his rags between him and the flint-strewn earth and the tarred sleepers, the lowered flaps of a wagon providing the sole protection at the sides. She both relished and was dismayed by the contrast between his condition and her own comfort, and she brooded about society's inequalities as she filled a gallon-sized stone ginger-beer bottle with boiling water, screwed the stopper in firmly, drew on a flannel jacket tailored to fit this improvised hot-water bottle, slipped it between the lavender-scented sheets, pulled up the fluffy Witney blankets, put the eiderdown in place, and then went downstairs to the kitchen to heat milk (served laced with whisky if anyone was suspected of an impending cold) and put out a tin of biscuits. If the fire had died down she would stir it with the poker and, with conscious extravagance, put a couple of lumps on it as she remarked: 'It's icy upstairs. We want to be warm before we go.'

That vagrant was, for her, a symbol of the terrible penalty of failure. She, and all of her type, knew that they must never be complacent; it was their habit to thank God for their good fortune as an insurance against punishment for taking anything for granted. Beyond those snug little houses, that regular job, lay peril to be avoided only by strictly moral conduct. For its own future protection the child was bombarded from many sides by moral precepts.

One day I learnt that all property was to be treated with respect. A neighbour's son, rather older than me, was drawing a face with chalk on the street side of a garden wall. I suppose it must have been an unusual occurrence or I would not have paused to watch him. Brick walls, anyway, did not provide a good surface for chalked graffiti. Little girls were accustomed to draw lines on the pavement for hopscotch, but these were removed periodically by housewives who, cleaning down their tiled front paths with hot water and a stiff broom, continued the process into the street. (A much-quoted proverb was: 'If each one swept before her door, the village would be clean.') Approaching on his daily walk was Mr Chambers, doyen of the Sunday promenade, indisputably the elder, sage and grand old man of the community. He needed no official position to enforce his authority; he was of an age when people, if respectable, automatically commanded obedience. No small boy, however unruly, would have presumed to answer him back. No adult would have

[64]

passed without greeting him and, if he was so inclined, staying to chat. Etiquette forbade reference to him as an 'old man'. He was 'an elderly gentleman' and he looked the part with his trimmed white beard, a rose in his lapel, a walking-stick. His house was, like all the others, in a terrace, but that thriving monkey-puzzle tree in the front garden somehow had the same effect as a flagpole; behind the clipped hedge and the closely cut grass it distinguished his house from the others and gave it the air of a superior residence. Prepared as I was for his greeting—he was elaborately courteous, even to children—I was surprised when he did not notice me but moved on a few paces, stood still, tapped his stick on the pavement, and waited until the boy with the chalk turned to face him. 'Got a bit of chalk, eh!' said Mr Chambers magisterially. 'And spoiling somebody's wall.' His tone left no doubt that this was a grave offence.

The culprit did not run away; local children could not, as in a crowded town, disappear into the anonymity of side streets and alleys. Every child was known by name to dozens of people. To vanish would have added another offence to one which was already serious enough. The boy squirmed with embarrassment, and made an ineffectual attempt to rub the chalk marks off the bricks with his sleeve. From now on he would be marked as on probation. Mr Chambers had 'spoken to' him, neighbours would tell his mother if she had not witnessed the public reprimand, and they would inform the owner of the wall. A child could be listed as a bad lot for anti-social conduct no worse than this.

For me this was a moment of enlightenment. I realized that walls do not simply occur. I saw that everything around me had been created, that it had cost money, that it belonged to somebody, and that the property of others was as important to them as our house was to us.

On this occasion the stability of society happened to be upheld by an elderly gentleman, but Mr Chambers was only one of many guardians of order. To a child in those days they were all around. Some of them were uniformed: tall policemen walking the streets at a measured pace, understood to be always available to carry a child off to a 'reformatory' if a parent's authority were flouted; the picturesquely-named rangers, tramping over the heath, formal in brown trilbies, brown jackets and knee breeches, polished gaiters and boots, whose mere appearance a quarter of a mile away was sufficient to cause small boys to scatter in case they were unwittingly contravening L.C.C. parks and open spaces regulations; the vicar, the living reminder that no peccadillo would ultimately go unpunished. Many more were not in uniform, but were none the less awe-inspiring: teachers, powerful figures at a time when fear was the main feeling inspired by schools; the school attendance officer who during school hours would accost children in the street or call at their homes if their absence was unexplained; adults in general, who were liable, like Mr Chambers, to admonish any child whose behaviour displeased them, or to offer well-meant advice such as: 'You ought not to be out in this cold weather without a coat on.'

Any occasion could provide the opportunity for instruction in right conduct, and it must be said that children accepted their role as apprentices to living. The impromptu lesson tended, in the right circumstances, to make a lasting impression. I still recall a day when my father and I, passing the Shooter's Hill fire-station, paused to look at the shining fire-engine, and a kindly fireman offered to show us the stables at the back. When we had been told the horses' names and had stroked their noses, he explained the drill for a turn-out. The brass helmets hung in a row where they could be conveniently grabbed by the firemen, and he remarked that they were polished every day whether they needed it or not; thus they were always smart and ready for use. Then, thoughtfully twirling a helmet on his fist, he went on to say that the principle behind this practice could be applied to many aspects of life. A simple routine, which took little time, ensured that whatever clothes you wore, whatever tools you used, were always ready when you needed them. I did not resent this moralizing; in fact, I warmed to it and—looking back over sixty years—I find it touching and significant that an ordinary fireman felt so secure in his philosophy as to talk like that.

All this conditioning was powerfully reinforced by books which were simply moral tracts. Books were expected to be 'improving', and for my mother this was their justification; she had a deep distrust of novels, which she classed with those paperbacks—purportedly written for servant girls—which were sold by newsagents and known as novelettes. Sometimes she would admit a novel if it were 'founded on fact'; but fiction written as entertainment she regarded as fraudulent. How could one spare time to read about people who had never existed or events which had never occurred? Her most damning criticism, applied to any imaginative work, was that it was 'far-fetched'. Apart from her bound volumes of *The*

Lady's World she did not contribute much to my Victorian reading, but she owned a few Sunday school and Band of Hope prizes. Even one of these, *Paradise Street*, she scoffed at as 'far-fetched', but she could not quarrel with the author's sentiments.

What she thought exaggerated about *Paradise Street* was the totally depraved condition of the residents at the start of the book and their regeneration. As depicted in the illustrations, the women wore cloth caps or hats with bedraggled finery, the men and the children were in rags. They fought, got drunk, stole, ran into debt, never washed—this was the extent of the vices which authors in this genre could bring themselves to mention. The kind of detail which Engels described so graphically in writing on poverty was missing here; Paradise Street, unless my memory betrays me, had no drainage problems. The inhabitants were sullenly hostile when new residents—a lady in reduced circumstances and her daughters—moved into the street, and they sneered as they saw the respectable furniture carried into the house. But a neighbour fell ill, and was surprised when the lady appeared with hot soup. Soup worked wonders on the Victorian poor, and the lady and her family were accorded the grudging credit of the street for the patient's recovery. By her unofficial social work, and above all by the example which she and her daughters set, the residents and the street were transformed. They ceased to fight or get drunk, they gave up crime, paid their debts and—washed and respectably dressed—they observed the Sabbath. Marxists would have regarded it as deplorable that such a work should have been placed in the hands of a young and impressionable child. The moral was that these slum-dwellers' degradation was the result of their own behaviour, that by copying a bourgeois model they could be better fed, clothed and housed. No trade union or militant political group intervened; they were able to revolutionize their surroundings simply by being prudent, respectable and moral.

I could accept this thesis because the most prized virtues during my childhood were thrift and foresight. Every Saturday morning hundreds of children made their way to The Hall which, for a few hours, housed the co-operative penny bank. A woman clerk sat at a trestle-table entering the deposits—mostly a penny but sometimes as much as sixpence—in the young depositors' passbooks; the atmosphere was as serious and decorous as in any ordinary bank. Annual interest at $2\frac{1}{2}$ per cent was added; it was a thrilling realization for a customer whose account reached £1 that he was credited with an extra sixpence, and at quite an early age children grasped the meaning of compound interest. They very soon knew, too, the importance to the household budget of the co-operative dividend on purchases; at that time it was around 1s. 6d in the pound and thus represented a rebate of 7½ per cent. The system has been much copied by other traders, but there was a significant difference then between co-operative dividend and trading stamps. The dividend was not declared until the annual trading results were known; when the profit went down the dividend dropped, and everybody was reminded that a business cannot pay out what it has not earned.

A still more powerful tract than *Paradise Street* was *The Moss Rose*, a very small book covered in a substance which felt disagreeably like lichen and smelt like a vault. The type was old enough to look alien to me, the pages were stained and limp, and it had an aura of sadness, but I could resist nothing, except the Bible, in print. I read it while I was ill and unable to go out, so to some extent I identified myself with the central figure, although he was a cripple who could not leave his wheelchair. Every morning his chair was pushed to the garden gate, so that his tiny world might be slightly enlarged. People spoke kind words to him as they passed and were rewarded with his sweet smile in return. When alone he studied the garden and became familiar with every plant in sight. As he could not play with other children, the flowers were his friends, and his particular pleasure was to watch, day by day, the gradual opening of a moss rose. I could realize his joy. All the men I knew loved their small gardens, which they had created themselves. Areas planted with seed became sacred ground; no child dared tread on them to recover a ball and dogs knew that a pawmark meant a scolding. From their earliest days plants were cosseted, worried over and admired. When my father came home on a summer evening his first concern was to look at the plants which were particularly on his mind; he could detect the slightest change in them. As a reader of Victorian stories, I knew that pleasure was paid for with pain; the fairest child was doomed to premature death and the long-awaited homecoming ship was sunk. As I read on I feared for the cripple's happiness, and wished that his pathetic short-term ambition to see the flower fully open might be realized. As I recall the story, the author prolonged the suspense. At last the flower was nearly out and the invalid was anticipating the culmination of his vigil. A strange boy, about to pass, paused to eye the flower. Guessing his intention, the cripple tried desperately to raise himself to prevent the unthinkable act. The stranger ignored him, casually picked the moss rose and walked on. Overstrained by his anguish and exertion, the cripple fell back into his chair. When the time came for him to be wheeled into the cottage he was dead.

It was a morbid little parable, calculated to start the ever-ready Victorian tears, yet its message was valid. You cannot estimate the value to them of other people's possessions. If you steal or destroy even the most trivial article belonging to somebody else, you cannot know the amount of the distress you are causing. Therefore there is no petty theft and theft is a contemptible crime.

Householders on the Estate would have read a further message into that story. Like the crippled boy's, their horizons were narrow. For most of their lives they alternated between home and workshop, their means were tiny and they reached their full potential early in life. They had no career structure offering them a step-up at intervals as they grew older. They were not buoyed up by the hope of sudden fortune; football pools did not exist. In these circumstances their pride and creativeness were expressed in their homes. They took an intense pleasure in a well-tended garden, an immaculate house, a new pair of curtains or a freshly-decorated room. They felt pain when newly-whitened front steps were sullied by unwanted callers with muddy boots, front doors scratched by gypsies with wicker baskets, cucumber frames broken by invisible urchins. They knew that the settler is at the mercy of the marauder, that the war between the producers and the wreckers is unending.

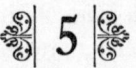

5

Nicht Hinauslehnen!

Among my mother's stock of stereotypes were some curt judgements on seaside resorts. Bournemouth was relaxing, Eastbourne (at least one end of it) select, Hastings too pebbly, Brighton crowded, Southend common, Clacton very exposed. Margate, however, was bracing, and that was what we needed. It was also easy to get to, being only about fifty miles away and, by train, reached quite comfortably in the course of a morning.

That we could go away for three weeks means that my parents must have managed their household budget with a good deal of prudence. Apart from Bank Holidays, industrial workers were not paid for holidays; if they wanted to go away, they had to take time off without pay. Accordingly, some men never had a holiday away from home; at best, the wife and children went to stay with relatives. Considering that the skilled men earned approximately the same wages, the differences in lifestyles were very marked. My father took the first week off to escort my mother and me to Margate; then he went back to work for a week, came down to Margate on the steamer for the middle weekend, and fetched us back at the final weekend. Compared with what the neighbours (except the school-teachers and Civil Servants) enjoyed, a holiday of this extent seemed lavish.

Many weeks before our departure I became aware of the magnitude of the project. Somebody had first to write to Mrs Hughes at Margate to confirm an arrangement already made the previous August. My mother would have liked to do this, but my father was uneasy about the dispatch with which she conducted correspondence—a rapid note dashed off with any pen which came to hand, a casual glance over it, an envelope addressed in an off-hand way, the whole procedure including the sealing and stamping completed in under five minutes. No misunderstandings every arose from her letters, none came back as incorrectly addressed, but my father felt that no task could be properly accomplished unless it entailed agonized effort.

When he wrote a letter he set time apart for the stages involved in such an undertaking. Having assembled the materials for writing, he held the bottle of Stephen's Blue-Black Ink against the light, peered at it critically, remarked that it seemed muddy and then looked round as though inviting an explanation. The last time he used the ink, he recalled, it had been perfectly clear. Accustomed to this opening move, my mother set her lips tightly and went on with her knitting. Then he examined the nib, invariably found it crossed and again looked round accusingly. A good thing, he would murmur just audibly enough for us to hear, that he had remembered to buy a new box. The box—the shape of a slim matchbox—was not on the shelf where he was sure he had put it, and he stood despairingly looking into a glass-fronted built-in cupboard. 'Right under your nose,' my mother would say quietly. The type of nib he favoured was the last of those mentioned in the famous advertisement: 'They come as a boon and a blessing to men, The Pickwick, the Owl and the Waverley pen.' He inserted the new nib in the penholder, moistened it between his lips (an unused nib would not take ink if dry), dipped it cautiously into the ink bottle so as not to stir up the mud, and then wrote 'Thames' several times on the back of an old envelope. The admired style in those days was copperplate; he had learnt it at school in the 1880s but children still had copybooks so that their handwriting would be formed in this style. His handwriting could well have been used as a model of copperplate and he wrote it at a fair speed. After this preliminary warm-up on 'Thames', and another frown at the muddy ink, he applied himself to the letter with the concentration of an engraver working on a precious metal. The slightest noise, or even movement, caused him to utter a gasp and glance in desperation at the ceiling. 'Nobody is allowed to breathe,' my mother would observe of these letter-writing periods. The result looked like a diploma rather than a letter. He read it through several times in case his eye had overlooked some trifling slip.

Still the tension was not relaxed. Now his full concentration had to be given to the envelope. The finished product had the perfection of a visiting card, but he scrutinized it anxiously, walked to the other side of the room, held it against the wall, and asked my mother: 'D'you think the postman will be able to read that?' Her invariable reply: 'He ought to be sacked if he can't!' never deterred him from repeating this procedure. Throats were now cleared, noses blown, there was a general air of relief, and he smiled as though we had all emerged from an ordeal. Usually he remarked on the high-quality gum on the Post Office stamps; he appreciated details like that.

Mrs Hughes's confirmation that our 'apartments' were available signalled the start of the preparations. The luggage standing in the spare room was inspected. The major piece was a black oval-topped trunk edged with brown leather and fitted at each end with strong leather handles; the base was reinforced with wooden slats; a massive lock at the front was of brass. The only trunks I have seen which compared with it in impressiveness belonged to an exiled Russian princess; hers, of course, were mauve, and adorned with a stencilled coronet above her initials. Ours was bourgeois rather than aristocratic, but it none the less evoked fantasies of shouting dark-skinned porters manhandling it on to a steamer under the eyes of its cheroot-smoking owner. Inside it was lined with a striped silky material, and it smelt of camphor. The minor piece of luggage was a long wicker basket reinforced with leather at the corners and fastened by a thick leather strap; it was strong and, like the trunk, very capacious. Both were dusted and, where necessary, polished.

It was usually at this stage that something happened which caused my expectations to sink. It might be that the trunk keys were not where my father had put them immediately after the previous holiday. Inanimate objects had a way of teasing him. 'I especially noted where I had put that,' he would say. The tool, book, receipt, stud, tie or whatever it was, carefully put in a place where it would be easy to find, simply dematerialized. 'I no sooner put a thing down than it disappears,' was the sentence which inaugurated a search in the most improbable places. Not until he had given up in despair would the missing object reappear in some prominent spot which it was difficult to overlook. As a rule, this phenomenon of the missing and reappearing article, although evidence of a malevolent universe, gave rise to no more than a passing irritation. But when it interrupted what should have been a sequence of smoothly-linked events culminating in, say, our going on holiday, then the entire plan stood in danger.

The keys were necessary to the trunk; the trunk could not be forwarded unlocked; therefore . . . I knew how his mind was leaping ahead, and mine kept pace with it. No train, no Mrs Hughes, no Margate sands. A search ensued, in which I half-heartedly joined. Meanwhile my father uttered such lamentations as: 'If only people would leave things where they are. . . .' If my mother overheard this accusation—the term 'people', after all, could apply only to those living in the house—she retorted that nobody had moved anything. Red in the face from the exertion of peering under the wardrobe and behind swaying piles of books and magazines, my father straightened himself and spoke the phrase I dreaded to hear:

'Set-back number one!'

The awful implication was that this was only the first of a long series of set-backs. Although he capably completed whatever job he undertook, he never expected anything to go right. As soon as the simplest outing was mooted, he at once foresaw and experienced in imagination practically all of the catastrophes listed in the small print of an insurance policy, except perhaps civil commotion. Yet he could not always have been like this. When single he had spent a long weekend in Holland with no more luggage than a clean collar and an extra handkerchief carried in a jacket pocket. On a holiday in Belgium, during the Boer War, he and a couple of friends were amused to see that the targets in a fair were effigies of Queen Victoria and the British generals. Seeing three obvious Englishmen competing with the natives in trying to knock these figures down, a puzzled crowd, apparently uncertain of the visitors' motives, gathered round. The British were unpopular on the Continent at that time, and had the onlookers suspected that they were being made fun of there might have been an ugly scene. This possibility had not troubled the three young men; they were all strong, my father said, and could have taken care of themselves. They had not been very much impressed by the Belgians.

Foreign travel was, of course, much simpler then. Passports were not required—he never had one, because he did not go abroad after the First World War—and there was no bother about foreign currency. The sovereign was respected everywhere, however much the imperialistic British may have been disliked; often they did not even need to change their money, because foreigners preferred it to their own. And it was unnecessary to book ahead. At a London terminus a passenger could buy a ticket, as easily as if he were going to Brighton, for practically anywhere that could be reached by railway. Even allowing for the lack of deterrent preliminaries, however, it was obvious that at one time he had not been a worrier. Something had happened to turn him into one, and I never knew what it was.

[73]

The trunk keys appeared, as inexplicably as they had disappeared. The trunk and the basket were moved into a position where my mother could put into them, after the washing and ironing, three weeks' supply of clothes—easily laundered clothing was still decades away. Hat-boxes holding several hats went into the trunk; I cannot recall that I ever saw my mother and father hatless in the open air, except in our garden on summer evenings, when they judged the sun to be not too strong. The trunk also held a collapsible stool, medicaments for emergencies, a sunshade, an umbrella, a walking-stick, and a spade and pail.

Set-backs two, three, four, five and six occurred, until my father lost count and merely remarked: 'Another set-back!' The cuffs of a shirt he wanted to take were found to be frayed; a rumour circulated that no unpaid leave would be permitted during August; I caught a cold which threatened to develop into something worse—one anxiety succeeded another. Sometimes it seemed surprising, so gloomy was the outlook, that the luggage continued to accumulate. I did not feel that our holiday was assured until my mother took out the Carter Paterson card from the middle drawer in the hall-stand.

That drawer contained not only this cheering token of a forthcoming holiday but also, to me, a terrifying *memento mori*. Among clothes-brushes and gloves lay my mother's burial insurance card, and I wished I had never asked the question which caused her to tell me. Her mother, with Victorian realism, insured all her eight children, for a penny a week each, against their funeral expenses. Although she would have liked to, my mother could never bring herself to discontinue these payments. She was obsessed with death, and 'saw the skull beneath the skin'. When death was mentioned, she spoke brusquely, forcing herself to face the horror. Mr Howarth, from the Prudential, called for the pennies at most of the houses in the street, including ours, and when I inquired why, my mother said in a scolding tone: 'That's money to bury me with when I'm dead.' As a child in Sunday school she had prayed to be taken up to heaven in a chariot and had hoped for years that she might become an exception to the general fate. The promise of that final certificate of respectability, a decent burial, seemed not to comfort her at all.

Carter Paterson's van, immensely high and pulled by a huge horse, was regarded by my mother as the main traffic hazard as it progressed through the streets on its weekly call. 'Mind you don't get under Carter Paterson's wheels,' was her final warning to me as I left the house. The driver, assisted by a boy who swung on a rope at the back with only his insteps making contact with the cart—his body formed an angle like a yachtsman when the boat is keeling over—looked out for the large 'C.P.' displayed in front windows. The boy knocked at the door, while the driver waited in his seat to see the size of the parcel. People stayed most of their lives in the same job in those days, and he was known to everybody as 'Carter Paterson'—for years I assumed that this was his name. 'My word, you've got something packed in here!' he said jovially, as he manœuvred the trunk through the front gate.

The evening before we were to leave my father bought the tickets at the station, in case there should be a delay at the booking-office in the morning. Traffic at the station was slight, but he envisaged a gigantic set-back caused by dozens of passengers arriving a few minutes ahead of us. Nobody was there in the evening except a few callers checking their watches with the station clock, and the station-master, also at that time acting as ticket clerk and porter, was glad of a chat.

Such was the importance attached to journeys that people dressed up for them, as though for a Sunday walk. My father wore a light-grey three-piece suit, with his silver watch-chain draped across the waistcoat, but his turnout differed from Sundays in that he wore a smart flat cap, which he thought suitable for travelling and practical in the strong seaside winds. In his hip pocket he had a brandy flask, and he carried a rug, although we were travelling in early August and unlikely to suffer from cold. I wore a sun-hat, a holland blouse with a striped tie, and grey shorts kept up with a belt fastened by a clasp in the form of a snake.

We had no luggage to encumber us, because it would be awaiting us at Margate, but getting out of the house, with my father in charge, was far from simple. Like an army unit about to embark, we had to be ready long before necessary. Nervous tension mounted as, with breakfast over, crockery washed up, the house in spick-and-span condition, we waited while my father went through a security routine. The Estate's immunity from crime did not tempt him to get slack. Window-catches upstairs and downstairs were tested, and he rattled the already locked and bolted back door. Leaking gas and flooding were his other fears. The gas taps were checked and double-checked although he had already shut the gas off at the meter. He inspected the water taps and turned them off tightly, but not so tightly that the washers might be damaged. His round would have been accomplished faster but for misgivings that at some point his attention had been superficial, and he would rush upstairs to repeat his precautions. My mother, who had been dressed ready to go for a considerable time, began to show impatience, but he was not finished until he was assured that he had everything he required on his person—handkerchiefs, a pipe, tobacco, matches, a penknife, a tiny magnifying glass, a watch, a watch key, a notebook, a very short sharpened pencil with a metal cap, a chamois leather sachet containing sovereigns, and the railway tickets. It was a moment of relief when the door opened and we emerged, but the ordeal was still not quite over. We had been trained that at this stage we must not say anything to confuse him; otherwise, as he put it, he was liable to 'get down the road and wonder whether I locked the front door'. Therefore we waited in silence while, with undisturbed concentration, he turned the key as far as it would go and gave the door some strong pushes to make sure that the lock would hold. Sometimes he re-opened the door, glanced along the passage, and then pulled the door to again.

Neighbours waved as we walked down the road and called out good wishes. My father's response was rather absent-minded; he muttered to us: 'We don't want to get ourselves held up', and urged us forward, his mind now set on getting us to the station. When we arrived there, long before the train was due, it was obvious that the staff took a more relaxed view of rail travel than we did. The booking-office was shut; the station-master's habit was to pop home occasionally between the infrequent trains and to reappear only a few minutes before the next train was due. The signalman, who also operated the level-crossing gates, could be seen drinking a mug of tea and reading a newspaper. The precaution of purchasing tickets overnight was clearly justified; without tickets my father would have suffered a nervous breakdown. Now he compared his watch with the station clock—he could not see a clock anywhere without checking his watch—and looked at the time-stained notices of the South-Eastern, Chatham and Dover Railway to assure himself that there had been no disturbing alterations in the timetable or the conditions of acceptance of parcels. The booking-hall, if it can be given such a grand name, had a dirty wooden floor and wooden walls painted in what had probably once been yellow, and it smelt of stale tobacco smoke; despite my mother's warning not to brush against the wall ('It's filthy') I savoured its dinginess, feeling that soot and grime were essential ingredients of the exciting nature of railways. I enjoyed, too, the dust-coated and chipped enamel signs advertising Stephen's Ink, Colman's Mustard, Monkey Brand, Bird's Custard, Pears' Soap, Beecham's Pills, Singer's Sewing Machines and Fry's Cocoa. Simple they may have been, but they had a way of embedding themselves in the mind. I studied them when, having crossed the line between the level-crossing gates, we waited on the down platform, and again and again I turned to the curious Monkey Brand advertisement, which showed a monkey grinning into a brilliant frying-pan above the warning: 'Won't wash clothes', and wondered why one was told what the product would not do.

The track ran in such a straight line that the smoke of the train as it left the preceding station could be seen. Looking at his watch, my father remarked approvingly that it was dead on time. The station-master now appeared, nodded amiably to us as though unaware that his absence from duty had caused head-shaking, and we all waited expectantly while my father warned us to stand back from the edge of the platform and not get into the train until it had stopped. We stood at the window as the train went over the level-crossing so that we could look at the little street of shops, locally known as the village, down which we had walked to the station. Then my father put the travelling rug on the rack, sat down and said: 'Well, we're off.' All those set-backs had been overcome, it was now up to the railway company to get us to Margate, and he was transformed into a happy man.

Railways offered three classes of accommodation. The first-class upholstery was blue and protected at head level by white, lace-edged antimacassars, the three ample seat places on either side were divided by arm rests, and the floor was carpeted. The second-class compartments were in a dull red and rather less spacious, but by modern standards they were quite opulent. My mother affected to despise second-class passengers—'Second class is no class' was one of her favourite aphorisms. We travelled third class, of course, as most people did, but no discomfort was involved; later I was to learn that foreigners landing at Dover and Folkestone obtained their first impression of British wealth from the fact that even the lowest-class compartments were upholstered. To me they indicated a vast, awe-inspiring world. The notice on the door read not only 'Do not lean out of the window' but also 'Ne pas se pencher au dehors' and

'Nicht hinauslehnen!' Beneath the racks were coloured scenes, usually a decade or so out of date, of resorts served by the railways: nineties ladies, under parasols, strolling along promenades; carriages —sometimes even a four-in-hand—waiting before grand hotels; piers, bandstands, ornamental flowerbeds, bowling-greens; yachts and paddle-steamers on an intensely blue sea. Yet, while leading the imagination to dwell on wide vistas, the railway provided an intimate glimpse into a world of little back gardens with chicken-runs, rabbit-hutches and beanpoles, small commercial hotels offering Good Stabling, the littered yards of hay and corn merchants, waiting horses harnessed to a brewer's dray, and tobacconists' shops advertising British Oak Shag. It was an unspectacular, drab but cosy part of north-east Kent through which we passed, but to a child from the newly-built Estate it was exotic and exciting.

Margate was the only other place that I came to know well, and therefore it was for me the alternative world. It was already well-developed as a popular seaside resort, but it was less the conventional attractions which thrilled me than the life of the town itself. Our daily walks to and from the beach took us near the gas works, a route my mother would have avoided if possible because a pungent smell permeated the area. Gas works were novel to me; I dawdled, appreciatively breathing in the polluted air. A narrow pathway between houses was surfaced in a material which gave off a metallic sound when walked upon; I stamped along there to increase the effect and stopped to listen to the sounds made by men with heavy boots. Most retail trade was carried on in small shops; shopping streets had not become standardized by multiple firms and they had the cheerful bustle of a market. Somehow I knew that my mother would not understand my appreciation of these mundane smells, sounds and sights, so I kept these pleasures to myself. I think I sensed in Margate an established town of natural growth.

As for the specific holiday pleasures, memory has stored those in a collection of tiny but very bright pictures: the row of brakes with striped awnings, and the clusters of sparrows beneath the horses' nosebags; the goat-drawn governess-cars; the group of saddled donkeys, their heads drooping as if in dejection; Lord George Sanger's Circus (my father, with his passion for getting everything right, was anxious that I should not think Sanger was a real lord); the huge, brown-sailed sailing ships which rolled alarmingly against the pier (as the owner waited to fill the boat, some passengers were sick even before the trip started); the curiously-named bathing machines, pulled to waist-high distance in the water by a carthorse; elaborate sandcastles built, mostly, by fathers, and surrounded by a canal system to facilitate their exciting destruction by the incoming tide; the man who walked along the sands every morning with a tray of hot Chelsea buns on his head; a shop with bubbling trays of faggots and another with sweet-making machinery in the window; a 'Professor Quinn' who gave diving exhibitions off the pier; and a 'lightning artist' painting landscapes. An evangelical group with a harmonium held children's services on the sands; the hearty singing could be heard the length of the promenade. One of the helpers, who approached my mother to ask if her little boy would like to join in, was given the dismissive look she assumed when answering the door to gypsies; open-air devotions, especially when accompanied by a lot of noise, offended her sense of decorum.

Strangely enough, my parents' roles as worrier and non-worrier were reversed on holiday. Freed of his obsessions about locking doors and turning off taps, my father became quietly genial. 'No need to hurry. We've got plenty of time,' he would say, half to himself. In the mornings he went for a swim; we saw him enter the bathing machine and then we saw him no more until he came down its steps and was again on the beach. In the evenings, dressed almost as for Sunday at home, we walked along the promenade or sat listening to the band. No view of workshops from the Peak darkened his thoughts on the way back to supper. My mother, however, had grounds for misgivings. The arrangement with Mrs Hughes was that she cooked and served the food bought by my mother. In the course of the holiday my mother accumulated objections against several shops, at which she would usually only hint: 'I don't care for the assistant in there'; 'They only look after their local customers'; 'I suspect you'd get a shock if you could see the rooms behind the shop'. She got irritable when I lingered before the faggots shop and refused to tell me what faggots were; all she would say was: 'You wouldn't like them.' Faggots were obviously something that, in her view, lowered the tone of the area. We had to avoid parts of the beach which the tide did not cover every day, because if you sat there you could 'pick up things'. We were wary about buying ice-cream—'You read awful stories about the places it's made in'—and we could not even venture to try unfamiliar brands of chocolate. Although her house had been chosen for its cleanliness,

[79]

our landlady was not trusted absolutely. When Mrs Hughes was out of the room after laying the table, my mother looked with apparent casualness at the crockery and cutlery and revealed her purpose only when she gave a plate or spoon an extra shine with her table napkin.

Margate as we knew it was still essentially a Victorian resort, but what was to come in the new century was being demonstrated by advertisers. A single-decker motor-bus, with seats facing inwards, drove slowly up and down the promenade. Its passengers, sitting with their backs to the windows, were girls with very long hair who were advertising, as the sign on the bus's sides showed, HARLENE HAIR DRILL. The motor-bus seemed to me a dingy vehicle compared with the brakes, drawn by beribboned horses, and the shining landaus waiting for hire, but the advertisers probably knew that the motor-bus, no less than the girls, would catch the public's eye. One year the *Daily Mail*, symbol of a new and audacious journalism as it was, advertised itself (and, simultaneously, two of its proprietor's enthusiasms, aviation and the Isle of Thanet) by a white monoplane with its name painted in black under the wings. While it flew at what would now be thought a dangerously low height along the edge of the beach, a photographer in the passenger's seat photographed the holiday-makers. A mood of exhilaration swept through the crowd, and they waved and cheered. Newsagents' shops showed the pictures on the following day, and persons whose heads were ringed in a white circle could claim an award.

During the last week the luggage again stood open to be packed with the three weeks' washing which now awaited my mother on her return home. 'Breathe in the ozone while you can. We shan't be able to breathe it for another year,' she would say as we arrived at the beach. She was determined that I should get the full effect of Margate's bracing qualities and occasionally, as an illustration of what the local air could do, she reminded me that I had first walked at Margate. At home I had shown no inclination even to crawl about; when my hands were held to encourage me to walk, I showed no interest. I had been content to sit still and contemplate the scene and I was not ambitious for promotion beyond the pushchair stage. One day, having been transported to the beach and settled down at my parents' feet, I stood up and walked. What was more, I walked back to our lodging, to the amazement of Mrs Hughes. Now, in the last few days, my mother would dwell on the passage of time and, in the spirit of 'Look thy last on all things lovely,' stand for a while contemplating the sea. I do not think she was really sad when Mrs Hughes, in turn, displayed a C.P. card and another Carter Paterson manhandled the trunk and remarked on its weight. It was a Victorian behaviour pattern to show melancholy at appropriate times. 'Isn't it nice to be in our own place again!' she said as soon as we arrived home. I did not share this view. The reality of the Estate (in our absence I had hoped that it might be magically transformed) brought a lump to my throat the moment we stepped out of the station, and during the remaining week of the school holiday I had to be persuaded to go out of the house.

When I did I encountered (the first time with incredulity) children who were spending their summer holidays on the Estate and apparently enjoying the experience. They were staying with relatives. Family relations, however remote, were cultivated then as a matter of obligation; regular correspondence went on even between relatives who did not particularly care for each other. The result was a network of contacts who could be visited for cheap holidays. If relatives lived at the seaside they were expected to endure annual visits; if not, any place made a change. When the post-holiday 'compositions' were written at school they told of holidays enthusiastically spent at such improbable resorts as Luton and Swindon; I felt sorry for those who had foregone the pleasures of sea and beach, but they had probably appreciated the ordinary features of those towns just as I had enjoyed the Margate gas works. The children (and adults) visiting the Estate spoke of themselves as having a country holiday, to the surprise of the residents, who regarded themselves as town-dwellers.

My parents were punctilious in keeping up with other branches of the family but we did not (in my mother's words) 'impose on each other'. That is to say, when we wanted holiday accommodation we did not go to relatives and we paid for it. Most of my mother's family lived in and around Reading which, although deficient in holiday attractions, had an advantage over Margate in that the dominant smell came from Huntley & Palmer's biscuit factory. The residents were accustomed to this aroma and barely noticed it, but to a visitor it suggested that all the town's housewives were busy over their ovens preparing for a gigantic celebration. The relatives and their homes were exciting, too, because—or so it seemed to me— they led lives in which they could do what they liked. Of course, they had obligations and restrictions of which I was unaware, and

[81]

which at that age I would not have understood anyway, but the difference between them and us was that they were economically self-contained. They did not 'go out to work'.

My mother's eldest sister, Rose, looking rather like Queen Alexandra, and no less regal in her bearing, received us in the rear room from which she directed the affairs of a thriving public house. What a contrast this establishment was to our quiet little house! Aunt Rose, sitting in her office, kept the books, stamped papers, signed chits, gave incisive answers to aproned men and women who came in through her always open door, and at the same time exchanged pleasantries with her visitors. She took us into the family's dining-room, where a sideboard so huge that it would never have got through the door of our house bore an enormous ham and a joint of beef, and a maid was laying the table. When, in reply to a question, I said I preferred to drink milk, I was given a pint glass full. Even my request to see a new pony, of which there had been some talk, was fulfilled at once despite a sharp shower at the time; Aunt Rose ordered that it should be brought into the kitchen, and there it was, tossing its head, shaking raindrops about, its hooves clicking on the red brick floor. Nothing impressed me with the expansiveness of this life so much as this matter-of-fact introduction of a pony into a kitchen; it was the nearest thing in real life to the appearance of a coach-and-six to take a pantomime Cinderella to the ball. Rose's husband, George, whose rubicund face was decorated with mutton-chop whiskers, had about him a Regency, horsy air; a good deal of his day was passed in an alcove in the bar talking senatorially with prosperous and responsible-looking men; he was, as it were, the front man of the undertaking. I remember his declaring that he never wanted to own a motor car, and adding: 'I like a good cob'. At that moment I envied him his stables, yard and paddock and the feeling of driving along country lanes, and I have never lost the nostalgia for an experience which I only fleetingly knew. Probably in my memory he has become a figure in a kind of Pickwickian romance, but the fact is that he enjoyed a more independent life than any of the men I knew; he did not need to fear Monday mornings.

All the seven sisters, except my mother, referred to their husbands by their surnames, and so did their mother. It was as though the men were the original members of firms which the women had been admitted to only later, but it seemed to be the women who kept a sharp eye on their businesses. I was aware that Aunt Rose was continuously alert, as if the establishment were a machine and she was listening to how it was running. Occasionally she commented on the noise of voices from the bar. 'It's quiet out there today. Everybody's at the . . .' and then she would name whatever event it was that accounted for the regulars' absence. At first I was only conscious that their conversation differed from the women's talk that I was accustomed to hear. No doubt there were times when they chatted about illnesses and knitting patterns but, when I came to understand them better, I realized that they were free of the Estate's inhibitions about discussing money. They surveyed the town's affairs not as people who just read paragraphs in the local paper but as insiders who knew all about who was making and who losing money, who was benefiting financially by deaths and marriages, what the vacant premises in the shopping street would fetch, who was going to oppose a street-widening plan. I listened avidly as though I were eavesdropping on an excitingly improper dialogue between some pretty fast characters, because the dominant theme was personal gain and back on the Estate I was being conditioned to regard that as wicked. My moral misgivings I kept to myself; these kindly and generous ladies, who made a flattering fuss of me, were surely innocent of any evil intent, and they did not fit the stereotype I was building up of the avaricious trader. It may seem improbable, and even absurd, that I felt ideological stresses at that stage, but I did. With disquiet I found myself wishing that my grandfather and his sons had stayed in their nice little pub in Rochester instead of going into that Victorian growth industry, engineering. If they had, I should not have been born on the Estate and not been taught to bother about the acquisitive society.

But my grandfather had not switched from The Ordnance Arms to industry because of any long-term calculation of financial prospects. He ceased to be a publican because his wife was on the way to becoming an alcoholic. Like his father who had chopped up the disputed rocking-horse, he was a man of high principles and prone to radical decisions. As an insurance against business failure he had (as was the practice then in prudent families) served an apprenticeship; people used to say : 'You'll never starve if you've got a trade in your hands.' He and his descendants never starved but they all had a touch of melancholy, as though they had missed their way.

6

The Right Time

When windows were open in summer, each hour was marked by chiming clocks; from every house, from front room and living-room they struck, as though from the towers of a distant town. Most evident were the deep traditional tones befitting the solemnity of time passing, but one neighbour's clock struck very rapidly on a high note, as if someone were irritably tapping a glass—I never saw this dissident clock, but I imagined it to be small and cheap. The community was obsessed with time, and the families we knew had, like us, clocks all over the house.

Our most important clock stood on the living-room mantelpiece, its pendulum swinging slowly; before striking, it whirred like the throat-clearing of a public speaker, and then—without any preliminary fancy chime (my father disliked clocks which imitated Big Ben; to him a clock was either Big Ben or it was not)—it struck with a startling resonance which sounded through the house; in the small hours, when I could not sleep, it was awesome. Some of the clocks—a brass carriage-clock and a dainty pink marble clock—were friendlier. The most frightening was a 'postman's alarm', a wall clock with a long pendulum; when the alarm was set (which was only on occasions of special importance) it went off with the shrillest, most brutal clanging ever devised by a clock-maker. All these clocks were kept going, but even if they should all, by a coincidence, have stopped, my father slept with his watch close to hand. That watch (which was supported by a reliable reserve) would probably that evening have been checked with those of time-obsessed friends, some if not all of whom had been to see the station clock—a commitment which could be pleasantly combined with exercising the dog and chatting over a pint at the neighbouring pub. The station-master was believed to receive the time on the railway telegraph system and at once, if necessary, to adjust the clock.

The men's watches were large and protected by lids which, when knobs were pressed, sprang open on one side to reveal the face and on the other to uncover the works. The owners seemed to get an aesthetic pleasure from watching the tiny machinery. 'This is a *good* watch,' they would say, and the way they said it implied not only that it was mechanically sound but that it possessed a moral virtue. Women's watches, however, were not taken seriously. Primarily ornamental, part of the owner's jewellery, they were worn pinned to the jacket—frivolous things, not to be regarded as proper timepieces. No child would ever have stopped a woman in the street to ask for the right time. Women often forgot to wind their watches; they were free of the masculine obsession with checking them. Women never stood in a group in the street, as men did, ensuring that their watches were synchronized. If asked the time, a man would say: 'Just a moment, I must consult my watch.' That word 'consult' indicated the reverence with which the watch was regarded. The overcoat and the jacket were then unbuttoned, the watch chain given a slight tug, the watch brought into view, sometimes even put to the ear to make sure that it was still ticking, the cover sprung open, the watch face solemnly gazed at before the pronouncement beginning: 'I make it. . . .' An elaborate formula was often used, such as: 'It wants just a minute to five-and-twenty past.' If the man had any companions, they would go through a similar routine, acting as though they were required to work out their bearings instead of simply to tell the time. Such occasions were an opportunity for reporting on a watch's condition, owner and watch achieving a complete identification. 'I'm afraid I must be gaining slightly,' or 'I seem to have lost a minute since yesterday evening.'

Apart from a bicycle, a man's watch was usually the most valuable single piece of equipment he possessed, and was identified with his history as an heirloom, a coming-of-age present, an investment made after qualifying in his trade and getting a skilled man's rate, a reward for long service. To emphasize a man's poverty, people would say: 'He hasn't even got a watch.' In these people's eyes the worst crime a thief could commit was to steal a watch. No replacement watch was ever a satisfactory substitute for the timepiece which had, when acquired, represented an achievement, which had been cared for over the years and trustingly consulted on innumerable occasions.

In a way, time was regarded as a local product, one of those British specialities, like guns and locomotives, for which the world looked to us. Greenwich was a name uttered with respect. On a summer afternoon visitors in straw hats, striped blazers, cummerbunds, walking-sticks, flowered hats, tight-waisted muslin dresses

and ankle-length pleated skirts would look up in awe at the dome
of the Royal Observatory as they climbed the hill, waiting for the
moment when the imposing clock came into view and the incontro-
vertible was revealed—Greenwich Mean Time. The words could
hardly be repeated without a tremor of emotion. In 1884 all the
maritime nations of the world had agreed to use Greenwich Mean
Time. That Britain should rule the time as well as practically everything else accorded with our most basic assumptions. For some while,
anxiously looking from my first watch to the Observatory clock, I
was confused by the 24-hour dial, but soon I was at one with the
fortunate people standing there whose watches were now in perfect
harmony with this master of all clocks. This was not the only privilege. Standing astride the line marking longitude 0, we knew
precisely where we were on the map.

A narrow path, bordered by a railing, runs along the side of the
Observatory, giving a view over the river and, to the left, of St
Paul's Cathedral. A walk on this path was a regular part of our
itinerary. One year (it must have been either 1910 or 1911) we
entered by the iron gate at the eastern end and saw a man in a light-
coloured suit and a panama hat looking through a long telescope
towards the Isle of Dogs. As he heard us approach he turned his
head sharply to look at us—we thought with an expression of annoyance—and we saw that he had a moustache with twisted turned-up
ends just like the Kaiser's. Then he clapped the telescope to and
strode away in the opposite direction. 'A German spy!' my mother
whispered. Her assumption was quite understandable, because in
magazine stories and children's comics spies tended to look like
stereotype Germans and to behave suspiciously. The mystery man
could, of course, have been a German; the Kaiser-type moustache
did not become popular here, perhaps because it typified the Kaiser,
but telescopes were not an unusual accessory—sometimes local residents, never suspected of being agents, peered through them from
the Peak and excitedly read the names of distant ships. He may
have feared, if a foreigner, that looking at industrial areas was forbidden, that we would denounce him and a hostile crowd would
collect. (Thirty years later, while on a security course, I wondered
whether he or his employers had perhaps hit on the idea that the
more you look and act like a spy the less likely the professional
counter-intelligence men are to suspect you.) Coming events cast
their shadows before, and my mother and her friends, without being

students of international politics, knew that some day we were going to fight the Germans.

It is paradoxical that although these people were so concerned with hours, minutes and even seconds, they would prodigally sign away theirs and their children's working lives. They lived in a liberal society where, in theory, they could offer themselves for any job within their capacity, actual or potential; in practice they behaved as though state direction of labour existed. When they thought of employment, they thought of people working in factories or offices; a few, specially favoured, were allowed to become schoolteachers because mechanics and clerks had to be able to read and write, but the rest must be glad to be employed rather than unemployed. Security was their overriding requirement, and, in the interests of attaining that, unhappiness—even misery—in work was accepted as the inescapable price. Awareness of that abyss into which the untrained, the improvident, could so easily slide never left them.

Children, of course, indulged their fantasies. The infant cinema, affording a weekly imaginative release into an exotic world, inspired countless would-be cowboys, but perhaps no event fired so many ambitions as did the arrest, in 1910, of the wife-murderer Dr Hawley Harvey Crippen and Miss Ethel Le Neve. In the eyes of the small boys on the Estate, the hero of this drama was the wireless-operator on the Canadian Pacific liner *Montrose* on which the doctor and his secretary-bookkeeper, in the guise of a 55-year-old Quebec business-man and his delicate sixteen-year-old son, sought to escape to Canada. What made the affair so sensational was its spectacular demonstration of the possibilities of wireless. Captain Kendall, the master of the *Montrose*, when two days out from Antwerp, was able to report his suspicions of the couple to his owners in Liverpool by a 'Marconigram' in time for a Scotland Yard detective to take a faster ship, the *Laurentic*, from Liverpool and head off Crippen at a point on the Canadian coast. Newspaper-readers could follow the daily progress of the two ships while Crippen and his fellow passengers on the *Montrose* remained ignorant of the world-wide excitement. For years afterwards—sensational stories did not just flare up and die but remained topical for a long time—boys tried to learn the Morse code, drew dots and dashes on the covers of exercise books, and tapped out messages on desks, window panes and dustbin lids. Wireless-operators, always nicknamed 'sparks', featured in stories for boys. Whether any students of the Morse code became wireless-operators I do not know; many would, if presented with the actual chance of such a job, have backed down on the grounds that they would not be able to get home to tea every day. Daring dreams of what they were going to do with their lives ended for most of them at the age of fourteen, or sixteen for the more fortunate, after which they could only speculate about what they might have been. So respectful were they of their elders that they could not have conceived how poor was the quality of the advice at their disposal. Any adult, when consulted, was prone to make such remarks as 'You want to be careful not to get into a dead-end job' or 'You want to get into something permanent'—clichés sound enough in their way but revealing no original thought applied to a specific case. No bank managers, accountants, family solicitors, doctors, company directors, no people whose occupations gave them an insight into other people's lives and business affairs, were available for professional or friendly consultation. The familiar middle-class fiddles by which sons are installed several rungs up an occupational ladder were not open to them. Parents had usually known nothing beyond their immediate wage-earning milieu. Mothers who had been domestic servants had seldom used their time of servitude as a reconnaissance into a more affluent class. Fathers, imagining themselves far-sighted, urged sons into apprenticeships within the narrow range of trades they knew about, on the assumption that those skills would always be in demand and those trades flourish unchanged. That the fourteen-year-old boy was being launched on half a century of bitter, clock-watching resentment occurred to nobody as worth mentioning. If any half-apprehended their fate they were reminded that life is no bed of roses or soothed by assurances that they would feel differently as soon as they started to earn money. Children were caused to invest their lives with less calculation, less sensible assessment of the pros and cons, less canvassing of informed opinion than a reasonable investor would have devoted to laying out £500.

Sadness underlay their exchange of pleasantries. 'You know what you ought to have been?' they would say by way of a compliment. The man addressed never replied that he was what he ought to have been, that he had shown engineering ability, survived an exacting apprenticeship, been accepted into the exclusive Amalgamated Society of Engineers, got a job which (although not pensionable) looked like being permanent, and now felt sure that he was doing what he was best fitted to do. 'What's that?' he would ask, preparing to smile modestly. He did not want to be told that he ought to be a foreman (that would have been intended and taken as an insult) or a workshop manager; he wanted no suggestions that he should be promoted in his own trade. He expected, and received, a tribute to something other than his engineering skill, to be told that he ought to have been a racing cyclist, a professional strong man, a concert baritone, a comedian ('You'd have made a fortune on the Halls!'), a politician, a landscape gardener. These were factory workers' dreams of what was going on beyond the workshop walls, a wistful realization that not everybody obeyed those orders which emptied the Estate of most of its male population every weekday morning. Men remarked, with a certain humorous wonderment, that when, while at work, they caught a glimpse of a street in midmorning or mid-afternoon, they were surprised to see quite a lot of men walking about. 'They can't all be on night shift or off sick. What are they doing out there?'

The question was often asked, and it usually led the inquirer on to the subject of 'cushy' jobs. The term applied to jobs on another level; it was at their own level, they were convinced, that the real work was done. All office work, from the lowest to top management, was without question 'cushy'; any attempt to justify it they dismissed as pretentious nonsense. They were not ambitious, or they professed not to be, to rise to such parasitical employment. They looked enviously downwards. They thought of the type of job which made scarcely any demands on the holder, which simply required his attendance and permitted him to pass periods in a state of snug semiconsciousness. Men taking their dogs for late-night walks paused to chat to a night-watchman who, guarding a road excavation, sat before his brazier boiling tea, frying sausages, smoking or just staring at the glowing coke. Having seen that his warning red lamps and guard ropes were in place, he could reckon on little traffic and no delinquency, could pass hours of being undisturbed. Stories were related of men who did nothing but periodically read pressures at the gas works, of gatekeepers who at infrequent intervals checked goods delivered to quiet little factories, of caretakers who could spend long hours in bed until the rare caller rang a bell. The point about all these jobs was that they were solitary, unobserved, unrushed, that they posed no problems to nag you in your free time; they were not unlike sitting outside an allotment toolshed at the weekend.

Such talk was indulged in when they were tired, discouraged and wanted to drop out. Animation lit up their faces, though, when they spoke of a life in the country. Then they seemed to feel that they had been called up for a spell of industrial work and would after a while be released back to the farmhouse where they belonged. A good deal of discussion was going on at that time about the promotion of smallholdings; in fact, an Act had been passed in 1907 to promote them, and Jesse Collings's phrase, 'Three acres and a cow', was much quoted. Yet the trend had been away from farming for decades, which should have prevented these practical men from being so starry-eyed about small farming. When they talked they conjured up visions of crowing roosters, clucking hens laying large brown eggs, fresh milk and vegetables, and friendly horses. Children's picture-books, songs about meadows and mill streams, supported this dream.

At the weekend my father liked to take a chair to the shady part of the garden, line up the family's footwear before him, and polish every boot, shoe and slipper to a showcase brilliance. He had a repertoire of songs which seemed to suit the rhythm of his brush-work, and the song I recall best went: 'Quack, quack, quack goes the pretty little duck, And the hen gives a cackle for a warning, And the old cock crows and everybody knows, There's an egg for your breakfast in the morning.' In between songs he would briefly lapse into a state of contemplation and, half to himself, repeat names. Canary Creeper. Morning Glory. Painted Ladies. Curly Kale. The sounds were exhilarating. It was easy to imagine a smallholding as an extension of this cosy little garden where my father could stay all day instead of going out to work. Yet on his bicycle rides into the country he must have passed little hells of damp bungalows, well water, dilapidated outbuildings, rusted wire-netting and mud. He often got into conversation with people, and chats with smallholders might have caused him to wonder whether the discipline of the market for agricultural produce was not even harsher than the routine of the armaments industry. On his mother's side he was only one generation away from farming. He simply remembered that his grandfather's life had not been spent (to use his own words) 'facing a whitewashed wall'.

It is odd that none of his circle ever contemplated starting a small manufacturing business. Technically they were well equipped to step out into this new age of mechanical development, to take advantage of this *Gründerzeit*. They knew the theory behind their skills, they could make and read machine drawings, their work required ingenuity and even inventiveness. Machines were not then repaired merely by inserting a spare part; the men who kept them running could themselves devise replacements. If they ever got animated about their work it was when they encountered a problem which needed solving; similar cases were recalled and sketches pencilled on scrap paper. It would not have been surprising if at least a few of the back gardens had contained little workshops where would-be inventors explored ideas, practical or fanciful, for improving the bicycle, cheapening the motor-cycle and car, mechanizing the kitchen and garden. They did not dream of attaining individual wealth, even by luck. Lotteries were local affairs promising a hamper or a bottle of port at Christmas. Magazine fiction-writers had to provide legacies from half-forgotten uncles in Australia to lift their characters to a more interesting level. Progress was going to make everybody better off. Those clocks, ticking and striking their lives away, were bringing not only Monday mornings but Saturday afternoons, and eventually a new age.

7

The Loftiest Heights

'We wish', Walter once wrote, 'to reach the loftiest heights to which our physical, mental and spiritual capabilities can attain.' He saw humanity as just emerging from a dark tunnel, filled with the smoke of the industrial revolution, into the bright sunshine of the early twentieth century. Humanity was riding in an electric tram.

The peak of the horse population had been passed in 1903, but the horse had by no means had its day. Nearly all local transport was still horse-drawn. Delivery horses, indeed, ranked among the local personalities, knowing as they did the customers and glancing expectantly towards front doors in anticipation of apples, carrots and lumps of sugar. Hay carts, brewers' drays, Carter Paterson's pantechnicons made their placid way along the main road; small boys would hang on the backs of these vehicles and other boys would shout to the driver: 'Whip behind, master!' Surely these carters must have been the last men in England to be addressed as 'master'. Some would casually flick the whip behind them and the boys would scatter; other drivers would take no notice and might even, from the way their heads rolled, have been asleep. Horses held children's imaginations. Two boys trotting in unison, their arms crossed behind their backs, were horses. Toyshops sold sets of harness for children to wear, and little girls knitted reins as presents.

Walter scorned horses, and used the expression horse-drawn pejoratively. Probably he did not care much for animals at all; progressives, in my experience, seldom keep pets, and I guess this is because animals' potentialities are limited and rapidly achieved, and they thrive best not on being harangued and organized but on simple affection. During his early years on the Estate he felt affronted by the existence, some three or four miles away, of horse trams—'an ancient line', he described it scornfully, 'with equally ancient horses and drivers, such as would delight the heart of an antiquarian.' Many of the local children were at one with the antiquarians; it was a treat to ride on the top, almost beside the driver, and see the horses below.

Electric trams were then not all that new. The first had run at Leytonstone, Essex, in 1882, and Walter felt that such a beneficial invention ought to be available, as of right, to every town-dweller in the country. Since 1906 he and others had been vigorously agitating for a local tram service. In that year the chairman of the Highways Committee of the London County Council had tried to assure a meeting that everything possible was being done but, as Walter observed, 'he was hardly definite enough in his statements'. The Council was bombarded with resolutions from what Walter called 'progressive bodies' and harassed by deputations until it capitulated. From his front bedroom window Walter was able to watch, with approval, the gangs of navvies tearing up the quiet road, laying two sets of rails, erecting huge iron posts to carry the overhead wires. Did he reflect that very soon, even late into the night and very early in the morning, noisy double-decker trams were going to grind past his house every few minutes, the passengers on the top deck staring into his front rooms and looking over the wall into part of his back garden? His watchfulness was directed not to the amenities of the environment but to the proper disposition of the stopping places. Two blocks were, he thought, the limit that anybody should have to walk. The day when the track opened was marked by a ceremony. A crowd collected at the terminus, speeches were made, and the first tram departed with its top deck occupied by official persons who cheered and waved to the public assembled along the route.

What he saw as the supreme triumph was the inauguration of a tram service along the Victoria Embankment. Just as railways brought civilization to the Far West, so trams were spreading democracy throughout London. A recital of how the Embankment was conquered found a place in many of his speeches. Two parties appeared in this drama, the rich and the workers. The rich, who had all spoken with one voice, had said: 'We don't want trams on the Embankment because we want to drive along there in our carriages.' The word carriages was an emotive one, no longer available to agitators. A present-day orator, wanting to convey the same effect, would probably have to say Rolls-Royces. The bicycle was the sole personal transport within most people's reach. Publicans and tradespeople might have a pony and trap, but only the rich had carriages. The workers had made the withering reply: 'We want to ride along the Embankment in *our* carriages.' There he paused dramatically, furiously agitating his coat-tails as the drama reached its climax.

Dropping his voice, speaking casually, he added: 'The workers' carriages were the trams.'

When the poor take over from the rich they seldom get quite what the rich enjoyed. Few people can have travelled on trams for pleasure. In their early days the top deck was open, and it was exciting to be up there, getting an all-round view and being brushed by the leaves of the plane trees bordering the road. But they were the primitive pioneering trams. Soon the tops were closed in, and the whole vehicle had an indescribably nauseating smell of hot metal and varnish which, combined with a swaying action and a rapid acceleration and deceleration, brought on the misery of tram-sickness. A common sight was a white-faced child hanging over the back of the conductor's platform in the despairing attitude of the bad sailor. Adults, having alighted, would draw several deep breaths and thank God that the journey was over. Later, more affluent generations may be puzzled that passengers did not simply get off when they felt ill; unlike sea voyages they were at any time only two minutes or so from solid land. The reason they stuck it out was that they could not bring themselves to sacrifice any part of the journey for which they had paid their fare. The fare-stage in those days was a halfpenny, and even the relatively prosperous would, unless pressed for time, walk the better part of a mile to cut a halfpenny off a penny fare. A halfpenny was worth saving, and thrift was in itself a virtue.

Of course, trams would have come soon enough anyway. They were cheap, capacious and fast. Within a few years they were to carry, day and night, thousands of munitions workers. The protram lobby might well have congratulated itself on its foresight. No doubt the ultimate decision to install the service was taken on the basis of transport experts' calculations of probable population growth, cost per passenger mile, and so on, but such were secondary considerations to tram enthusiasts, who saw them, like the Estate, as part of the realization of an ideal. The quality the London tram possessed which buses and the railway lacked was that it was publicly owned. To collectivists it was beyond argument that publicly-owned transport was better, of its very nature, than services operated by profit-seeking companies. People to whom a municipal tram and a capitalist bus were simply modes of getting passengers to their destinations were unenlightened, unable to distinguish between good and evil, incapable of feeling the moral glow of those who refused to hail a bus and virtuously waited for a tram. The faithful even looked askance at anyone who criticized the trams, fearing that if the slightest fault were conceded the way was open to a condemnation of the whole system. At an early age Walter's pupils were introduced to municipal finance because of his anxiety to refute allegations by the opponents of municipalization that the trams lost money. He explained that the apparent loss arose from a difference in book-keeping practice between a municipality and a limited company. Probably none of the children who looked at him so earnestly understood his explanation but they gathered that the workers' enemies were up to all kinds of tricks.

The trams had opened up London to the Estate. As Walter not infrequently remarked, our own transport could now take us, at a fare everybody could afford, to enjoy the wealth of the picture galleries and museums—he saw London as consisting largely of places for improving the mind. It was an idyllic picture of respectable citizens, 'splendid in their public ways', seeking culture. Parties, led by art and history teachers, did in fact occasionally travel to London and, having triumphed over tram-sickness and the tedium of the journey, returned to hold discussions on what they had learnt.

One Whitsun, however, Estate residents became aware that the Estate had also been opened up to London. The London County Council, in the spirit of municipal enterprise which was constantly being urged upon it, had advertised cheap trips to the countryside and woods which the Estate adjoined. The poor of south-east London took advantage of the offer in enormous numbers. From an early hour, noisy tramloads of them arrived at the usually quiet terminus. Some were content to sink down on the dusty banks at the foot of a steep hill leading to the heath and the open country beyond, and wait for the pubs outside the Estate boundary to open. Their children, unwilling to be so inactive, meanwhile raided the front gardens in the immediate area; if this action did not result in a tragedy comparable to that which had so moved me in *The Moss Rose*, it none the less caused murderous rage in householders' hearts. It revealed a hitherto unimagined menace; the local dirty kids would never have contemplated such a crime. Fortunately the invaders did not penetrate far into the Estate, but what was spared the Estate was inflicted upon the heath. On the Monday evening, when the packed trams were taking the strangers away, the residents went out to inspect the damage. Public benches, where not fixed in concrete, had been thrown about and smashed. Saplings had been uprooted,

bushes set on fire, and rhododendrons—then in bloom—torn to the
ground. A policeman stood before a clump of despoiled bushes, vainly
guarding them after the damage was done. Little groups, dressed as
usual for the evening walk, stood about, looking sorrowfully at the
waste paper and empty bottles, discussing the devastation. My
mother, trying to be tolerant, remarked that the poor things never
saw a blade of grass, but few were inclined to understand, and our
neighbours prescribed flogging, imprisonment with hard labour, or
conscription. Old fears of the London mob, of ruffians, toughs, bullies
had been aroused. No event so shocked the little community as did
this raid from the slums, this demonstration that increased democracy did not mean uplift all the way.

It added to the mental confusion of the young who were being in-
doctrinated in the Estate's prevailing ideology. Taught to be proud of
being working class, they found themselves feeling immensely
superior to these proletarians who had ravaged the heath. Where
did they themselves stand in the social structure? Fiction-writers
seemed to know, apart from paupers and tramps, only two classes:
down below were humble cottagers, servants, gamekeepers, cabbies;
above were children with nurses, comic mademoiselles and Fräuleins,
ponies, gracious mothers who made brief appearances in the nursery,
fathers who retired to studies, were driven to offices, shot pheasants,
landed monster salmon, raised grey toppers as the royal horse flashed
first past the post, reverently handled a cobwebbed bottle of port
brought up from the cellar. Even popular newspapers expressed surprise that households could be run without servants. One of our
family jokes arose from a newspaper paragraph about a Labour M.P.
named Will Crooks. Crooks was not a flamboyant figure; his politics
were homely, and he seems to be little remembered now. Some writers
on the early Labour movement do not mention him, but at the time
he was regarded as a considerable portent. On one occasion he entertained some distinguished visitors in his tiny terraced house in the
East End, and journalists wonderingly reported that: 'Mrs Crooks
prepared tea with her own hands.' The editor who allowed that
sentence into his paper can have had no idea of the hilarity it caused.
'Instead of with her feet, as you would expect,' my mother commented. 'Believe it or not, I am now about to prepare tea with my
own hands.'

The horrified reaction when the church-going Mrs Perry sent her
fourteen-year-old Molly 'into service' probably occurred because it

typed everybody else as belonging to the servant class. My mother was appalled. 'Molly's being sent away as a skivvy,' she announced at tea. Her announcements of local sensational stories were usually made at tea, a leisurely meal. All I remember of that conversation is my father's expression at that emotive word 'skivvy' and his conviction that Mr Perry could not have approved. Similar conversations were certainly going on at other tea-tables. Perhaps surprised by the general hostility, Mrs Perry croaked angrily to the effect that service in a big house—and Molly was going to 'a castle in Wales'—was the best education a girl could have.

Within a week of Molly's departure my mother made another exciting announcement. Molly was back. As soon as she learnt what was expected of her she left. It was a courageous act for a young girl, and there were tearful days after her return, but it was a victory. Yet, although no further attempt was made to send her into service, she felt as scarred as though she had been to prison. The subject was banned from discussion and no new acquaintances were told. She was back on our island, parading across the heath after church, arm in arm with her girl friend, their white-gloved hands clasped. The castle in Wales was a long way away and Molly was a young lady once more. Soon hitherto undreamt-of avenues of employment were to open, and no girl of Molly's class would ever again be sent into service.

8

The Stuff to Give 'Em

Long before 1914 a pack of 'snap' cards contained a pair of pictures depicting a goosestepping German soldier in spiked helmet, grey uniform and top boots, his red face adorned with moustaches like the Kaiser's. From his fixed bayonet dangled a string of sausages and from his side pocket protruded a document entitled 'Map of England'. In homes where children played this version of the game the figure must have personified the Germans—ridiculous but menacing. Had capitalist imperialism been as all-powerful, as cunning and far-sighted as its opponents supposed, this comic German infantryman might have been introduced into the pack to condition British youth to the idea of an inevitable war against an aggressor whose defeat would present no great problem. The production of playing-cards, however, being part of a chaotic system in which manufacturers simply turned out what they thought they could sell, the probability is that the artist innocently drew the would-be invader in the same spirit as he portrayed butchers, bakers and sweeps—an immediately recognizable character likely to arouse infant amusement. In the ordinary person's stereotype of Europe, the Germans had been cast in a familiar role of enemy. No pack of cards showed any other nation's soldiers marching towards England.

In July 1914 army waggons drawn by horses and mules, gun teams and motor-lorries appeared on the main road making their way to a newly-established camp on the marshes. A road across the marshes, usually deserted, became a promenade for families and groups of laughing girls. To children too young to remember the Boer War the soldiers' khaki was disappointing, as it lacked the dash and glitter of the red and blue uniforms worn on church parades. But the bell tents, the lines of horses and mules, the limber waggons, the military domesticity—khaki shirts hung to dry, soldiers shaving outside tents in preparation for a swaggering stroll and a pint—the smell of smoke and bruised grass, suggested a fair. At dusk thick, cream-coloured searchlight beams moved across the sky.

At home the usual pleasurable excitement of packing for our holiday at Margate was intensified by my father's decision to buy a new house. For as long as I could remember we had, while out walking, looked at houses being built. No one, in my recollection, ever deplored the spread of suburbs to the country; rather was it a sign of progress that people could move to cleaner air and pleasanter surroundings. We seem to have supposed that we would remain on the border between London and Kent instead of being overtaken by London's expansion. Time and again we had passed a new row of houses and looked at the end one, which had a garden three times the size of ours, a wide side entrance, upstairs a bathroom and lavatory, and—height of elegance—french windows opening on to the garden. It cost £275, paid in cash, for a 99-year lease. Houses were built solidly in those days—even the party walls were of brick—and purchasers were not expected to move in and put faults right afterwards. The house stood empty for months, while fires burned in the fireplaces to dry it out. Periodically the works foreman and my father went over it thoroughly, climbing in the loft to inspect the roof, peering for cracks in ceilings and walls, testing that windows functioned properly without sticking or rattling, swinging doors and trying locks. The slightest defect was corrected as a matter of course; the foreman was no less critical than my father. Inside decoration did not begin until both parties agreed that the house was now habitable.

But that summer occupation of the house was a distant pleasure, whereas the stay at Margate was imminent. If it occurred to my father that troop mobilization might presage the greatest set-back ever, he kept his fears from me. On a bright Sunday evening before the August Bank Holiday we walked to the camp on the marshes. The crowd moved slowly, with the customary pauses for greetings, and laughed at such spectacles as a soldier washing his face in a bucket and two soldiers clowning—one holding a tiny looking glass while another, a large man, peered in it to comb his hair. An acquaintance, strolling with his family, nodded to my father and said while passing: 'We're going in tomorrow, Jack.' No private houses locally had telephones; before radio the Government had no means of instant communication with the population. News that the Bank Holiday was cancelled, that munitions production was immediately going on to a war level, was passed by word of mouth. Not one man was missing the following morning when the first twelve-hour shift began.

My strongest recollections of the early days of the Great War are not of objective events but of a trance state into which the world seemed to have submerged. Suddenly, from unfathomable depths, welled up imagery, legend, fable and prophecy. Already an avid newspaper-reader, I studied the cartoons, and their message was repeated by schoolteachers, tram passengers, housewives over garden fences, the choir-mistress rehearsing in the vestry and the vicar in the pulpit, all of whom saw the conflict as fought on a higher plane by fabulous beasts and magic symbols. The British lion, hitherto envisaged as calmly gazing out to sea, its front paws comfortably crossed, a patient and lovable beast, now stirred, growled, sometimes roared; the king of the jungle, superbly self-confident in the knowledge of its superior strength, could not be defeated. The bulldog, solid, squat, tenacious, stood on the cliffs of Dover, baring its teeth. Unlike primitive peoples, the British did not equip themselves for war with bulls' horns or leopard skins, they did not paint fearsome creatures on their weapons, but their spirits found reassurance in imagining that they, in some mystical way, possessed the qualities of lions and bulldogs. The Gallic cock, less solid and powerful, had colourful plumage and a fighting spirit; if we were not too sure of its weight, we were comforted by the presence on the other side of Europe of the Russian bear, rearing on its hind legs, extending its massive forepaws, baring its terrible fangs. Threatening these archetypal creatures was the Prussian eagle, a predator hovering with wings wide spread, curved beak ready to strike, talons half-clenched. Human symbols also assumed reality. Britannia, a calm, matronly figure, affectionately familiar from her portrait on the penny, watched over the seas. John Bull, with piercing eyes and set jaw, perhaps too portly to be regarded as a combatant, embodied our wealth and authority; his function was to mete out judgements and punishments, to deal with the Germans as though they were a wayward tribe. St George, forever slaying the dragon on our sovereigns, was pictured ready to hand out similar treatment to the enemy. The French Marianne, chic in a tricorne, tight bodice and wide tricolour skirt, was an object for our chivalrous concern. Ivan, the uniformed peasant, was unstoppable once, with fixed bayonet, he started to move forward. Germany was represented not by the slightly bemused flour-miller, Michel, but by the Kaiser, a monster of frightfulness (a much-used description), stalking with blood-dripping fingers over battlefields and ruined villages, sometimes attended by the comic figure of the Crown Prince, 'Little Willy'.

A state of euphoria prevailed, as if something marvellous had happened. Coronation flags reappeared in front windows. Passing groups of soldiers broke into spontaneous waving and cheering. It even seemed at times as though everybody were participating in an enormous joke. N.C.O.s in charge of marching parties yelled the order: 'Eyes—left!' as they passed a girl on the pavement or at a front gate, and naughty grins appeared.

Yet fear accompanied the exultation. On the Tuesday after the Bank Holiday the co-operative stores (known to us simply as 'the stores' to distinguish it from other shops) presented an astonishing spectacle. Built to a design common in those days, it had a grocery counter on the left as you entered, a provisions counter on the right, and what was called the corn counter at the end. The male assistants, who worked sixty hours a week, wore white aprons from neck to ankles. The senior men occupied the positions nearest the door; the others' status diminished with their distance from the door and arrived at the lowest grade with two boys on the corn counter. Their skills lay principally in weighing and wrapping, because most products arrived in bulk. Butter came in huge blocks; an assistant scooped out an approximate quantity, beat it into shape, weighed it and added or subtracted small quantities. Tea, biscuits, sugar, sweets, flour were all weighed and packed before customers' eyes. Under the counter were bags, blue and brown paper; above, convenient to the hand, hung a ball of string. Assistants developed a conjuror's dexterity as they twisted 'screws' and converted assorted awkward packages into handy parcels. It was a slow method of shopping which favoured the pushing customer, and the long waits caused gossiping groups to form and obstruct other customers' movement. After the packing the assistant took the money, gave change, and wrote the amount of the purchase on a small slip which the customer then exchanged at a small office staffed by a bad-tempered girl (the only female in the department) for metal dividend tokens known as 'tin checks'.

On this occasion I arrived at midday at the stores with a routine list. At the far end assistants stood about idly. Shelves, hitherto always crowded with goods, were bare, and familiar jars and tins stood empty. A few voluble customers congregated at the door end of the grocery counter. Mystified, I took my place behind a smaller boy who also held a list. As he read off the items the assistant said 'Sold out' and I mentally crossed them off too. Finally the boy asked:

'Have you got any salt?' The man said: 'Hope so, son!' and raised a general laugh.

This incident did not accord with the prevalent jubilation. Nor did the sight of the trunk and wicker basket being unpacked. Throughout each year our three weeks at Margate had been my horizon. I had appreciated every hour of it; not only the sea, the sands, the pier, the bands, the four-horse brakes and Lord George Sanger, but the town itself. My attitude to the place where I was born had never been more critical.

Then another blow fell. I was not to spend the rest of the holiday wandering over the heath, watching the soldiers, or reading old magazines in the lumber-room. With over three weeks' holiday still to run, the schools re-opened. I never heard an explanation of this decision which seemed to me rational. I remained sceptical until the school bell rang and I saw children moving up the road. Having got to school, I could not believe that the dismal routine of prayers, lessons and playtime could go on in August, but it proceeded as though the calendar had moved forward into September. The sole absentees were the boy scouts, who went into uniform and let it be known that they were on duty guarding bridges. Some time was to elapse before the authorities realized that the only bridge in the vicinity was the footbridge over the railway line at the station. In default of any other bridge requiring protection, it was this which the scouts—equipped with poles, bugles and whistles—were guarding. They had made the useful discovery that you can get away with anything, however idiotic, if you claim to be acting in the interest of national security.

Maps of the Continent, with movable flags for plotting the Allied advance, appeared on classroom walls. We looked forward to moving the British and French flags eastwards, and we were given such encouraging information as the distance in miles between our troops and Berlin. The undeniable fact that the German army was much larger than the British was swept aside, by otherwise quite sensible people, with the assertion that one British soldier was worth five German soldiers—an equation which still left Britain's 750,000 regulars and territorials unequal to the German force of five million. But add the white populations of the Empire and the millions represented on the missionary posters, potential Christians and now potential soldiers, all grateful to the mother country and anxious to serve, and our land superiority was immense. Everybody but R.S.M. Empson seemed to have forgotten how the Boer War had dragged on for years. Talk about getting the Hun on the run went on among men who knew more about guns and ammunition than most people did. They knew the range and power of the armaments they were turning out, and they must have realized that the Krupp works were no less capable of mass-producing lethal devices. Nobody could have supposed that it took five times as much explosive to kill an Englishman as it did a German. Indeed, many people, ignoring artillery, saw the war in terms of hand-to-hand combats. 'The Hun doesn't like cold steel. Just give our lads the chance to get at them with the bayonet.' Adults said it, children repeated it, and they flocked to the heath to see the rehearsals for these decisive encounters.

One side of the heath had been wired in, long creosoted wooden huts erected, practice trenches dug, and what then remained of the grass trampled bare. Squads fell in, dressed by the right, stood at ease, came to attention but not smartly enough, came to attention again and this time put a bit of snap into it, formed fours. Schoolchildren, errand boys with bicycles, housewives with prams, and elderly men stood outside the wire to watch the novel spectacle until, elsewhere on the field, bayonet practice began, when they moved to this more warlike scene. The soldiers were in shirt-sleeve order; their collarless shirts made them took like navvies. Other Ranks had no collars and were thus clearly designated as proletarians. As befitted their one-fifth rating, German soldiers were represented by hanging straw-filled sacks. The men charged these, shouting and leaping a narrow trench on the way. 'In! Out! On guard!' the instructor yelled as his pupils punctured the sacks. A lithe man, hatless and wearing a white sweater and dark trousers, he sprang about nimbly, taunting the panting and sweating men. They seemed to him to need a dose of Mother Seigel's Syrup (a widely-advertised tonic). Next time he wanted to *hear* them shouting, he wanted to *hear* them grunt. 'It's you or him!' The spectators laughed.

Everybody was supposed to enjoy the war. Soldiers were portrayed as though they were on an organized holiday. A greengrocer presented a load of bananas to troops in Regent's Park; as they marched past his shop the men sang, to the tune of 'John Brown's Body', 'Thank you very much for your bananas.' A Kentish farmer invited soldiers to eat the apples in his orchard. Householders asked soldiers far from home to share their Sunday dinner or tea. Cinemas admitted men in uniform free. Newspapers gave prominence to items like these. The catch phrase 'That's the stuff to give the troops!' summed up the idea that luxuries were heaped upon them; parcels followed them as far as the trenches—pictures showed jolly Tommies, surrounded by neat sandbags, rejoicing over fruit-cakes, jars of marmalade and woollen scarves. According to journalists, men 'had the good fortune' to be sent on active service. Even the severely wounded were lucky; a 'Blighty one' brought them back home, to be photographed giving the thumbs-up sign and fussed over by gracious society V.A.D.s.

If anyone formed the civilian's view of the front, it was surely the cartoonist Captain Bruce Bairnsfather. His principal characters, contrasting in Laurel and Hardy fashion, were the imperturbable walrus-moustached veteran, Old Bill, and his smaller, and sometimes apprehensive, companion Bert. Bairnsfather's drawings appear realistic, with their waterlogged shell holes, dugouts, splintered tree stumps, and ruined houses and barns, yet there is a cosiness about the scenes. Frequently the pair appear to have the front to themselves. Old Bill dominates his surroundings, untroubled by superiors, as impervious to steel and explosive as a film hero. You feel that, despite the couple's moans about the shelling and the arrival of even more unwanted plum and apple jam, rum and hot soup are never very far away. No situation arises which a sardonic remark cannot make bearable, and the enemy is always ridiculous. They are an upgraded version of the tramps in children's comics who, although ragged and homeless, are not really lousy, cold and hungry, but who live well by artfully snatching the huge pie which the fat cook has made for the policeman. Old Bill and Bert did not appear crudely depicted in a halfpenny comic but in elegant wash-drawings printed on glossy paper; issued as collections between covers, these took their place among Christmas annuals and were looked at again and again.

The village, not usually an exhilarating thoroughfare, now provided occasional excitements. Troop trains stopped at the station and soldiers alighted, fell in in fours, answered a roll call, and then marched, panting under their heavy kit, up the steep hill to the huts on the heath. The Estate rapidly formed an opinion of each new intake. The West Kents and Gloucesters were 'gentlemen', but a kilted regiment was looked at with astonishment. Scotland was thought to be romantic, peopled with colourful characters like the officer on the Camp Coffee bottle and not by stunted, skinny men with pinched faces and a general air of dejection, products of generations of under-nourishment. Later came Australians, men who seemed giants to the Estate dwellers, among whom a man six feet tall was a rarity. The Australians were more noticeable than other troops not only because of their physique and hats but because of their habit of lounging about; they sat on kerbs, windowsills, doorsteps and walls; they lay and even slept on grass verges, and they huddled in groups on any patch of grass and, quite openly, played cards for money—a flouting of the law which attracted as spectators groups of awe-struck small boys, to whom they threw pennies. It is safe to say that no one locally had ever before been seen to throw pennies about. But whoever the soldiers were, they turned out in hundreds in the evenings to walk, again and again, the length of the road across the heath. To them it must have seemed desolate without a bar, café, coffee-stall or cinema, but in the twilight the glowing ends and the smell of hundreds of Woodbines, the clatter of army boots and the strange voices, an occasional illuminated face as men drew on cigarettes, were for schoolboys a glimpse of the drama of war and of adult life. Mysterious women appeared, of a type never seen on the Estate; smoking in an ostentatious manner—it was still rare, early in the war, for women to smoke—they hung about on the edge of the dark woods.

Periodically the heath reverted to its normal weekday loneliness. In darkness the troops marched to the station and went away on the line which had taken us to Margate; doubtless the funny men among them joked about 'Nicht hinauslehnen !'.

The heath acquired permanent military inhabitants when a searchlight and anti-aircraft gun station was set up. It was a simple compound, enclosed by a few strands of barbed wire. No sentry was posted, no 'Keep Out' notices erected; the crews were quiet, friendly men, glad to talk to evening strollers. They made the place homely with small flowerbeds and smells of cooking. For local residents they were an object of pride, as though they were the home team.

Zeppelin raids became—as no bombs fell near the Estate—an enjoyable participation in military action without much risk. The airships' speed gave the people below time, after the warning siren had sounded, to dress, go downstairs and put the kettle on for tea. This stirring at an unusual hour caused dogs to bark and cocks to crow. People threw up windows, looked out from dark rooms, and told each other than the 'Zepp' must have just crossed the coast. The first distant gunfire was little more than a faint tremor in the air.

We turned the gas out, pulled the blinds aside, and watched the searchlights probing the area downriver until they picked up the raider, a tiny object of brilliant silver. As the gunfire grew in intensity the surrounding woods became alive with bird noises. In summer the sharp crack of the shells stimulated nightingales; a powerful solo by one bird developed into a duet until the night was thrillingly full of gunfire and birdsong. The next morning people spoke as much of the nightingales as of the raids.

Always a rumour centre, the barber's shop was now enlivened by exchanges of supposedly secret information. The barber, who wore a very obvious wig (customers suspected that he was totally bald and thus never needed another barber to cut his hair), was a church-warden, but his shop had a raffish air. Frosted glass over the lower two-thirds of his window space, preventing passers-by from seeing anything but tins of pomade on a top shelf, suggested a masculine enclave, and this impression was reinforced in the smoky interior by racing and boxing prints and the hint of another manly sport in the coloured posters depicting knuts and mashers whose luxuriant hair and moustaches had been promoted by the pomade. Waiting customers who had failed to secure a copy of *Titbits* or *Answers* (limp and smudged from months of handling) could also stare at framed colour prints of shirt-sleeved, cigar-smoking black billiard-players and try to puzzle out the phonetically spelt words in the balloons emerging from their mouths. Darkies, coons, dusky beaux and belles were standard funny characters of the period, laughed at even when not understood.

While the customers were talking, however, no distractions were needed. What in the Second World War was to be called careless talk was unrestricted. Knowing looks, head-shakings, judicial pipe-puffing accompanied every rumour about the destination of the troops encamped locally, armaments production, food supplies, the possible introduction of women workers to replace men (unanimously deplored) and the scandal of the continued availability of German-made goods. Apparently to everybody's surprise, British shops and homes were found to be harbouring sewing machines, household utensils, razors and toys of German manufacture, and—most sinister of all—picture postcards. That presses in Saxony had printed coloured views of the piers, promenades, bandstands, jubilee memorials and ornamental gardens of English seaside resorts was held to be evidence of the extent of pre-1914 espionage. What should be done with these

now tainted goods was never decided. Should one refuse to buy a
Solingen razor and demand one manufactured in Sheffield? What
about the Solingen razor one owned already? As for espionage, even
the Kaiser himself had engaged in it. The newsreel (called the
Topical Budget) shown at the Wesleyan Central Hall revived memories of a state visit by the Kaiser to London. He was shown riding,
with the puppet-like movements of the early cinema, beside King
George V. His glances to each side of the street, and occasionally upwards (presumably to acknowledge cheers and waving from spectators at upper windows), were interpreted by the booing and hissing
audience as the actions of a man noting details of the metropolis.
All these topics provided the customer with anecdotes to retail, but
the barber, although a good listener, failed to voice the downright
opinions which put fire into a discussion.

The place for emotion was the fish shop run by Mrs Ross. Though
customers spent less time there than at the barber's, they came
away much more depressed, indignant or filled with patriotic fervour
and confidence than if they had been to a public demonstration.
There was a Mr Ross too, but he did the rough work such as fetch-
ing the fish-boxes from the station and unloading, which gave him
little contact with customers; sales and public relations were
handled exclusively by his brawny-armed wife. The Ross shop,
which enjoyed a local monopoly of fish, was noted for bloaters; she
meticulously asked people whether they wanted hard or soft roes
and nipped the fish in a way that caused the roe to ooze out. Un-
asked, she added a commentary on the day's news and vast generali-
zations about nations, countries and continents. The French were
particular objects of her scorn, largely, it seemed, because of reports
about the relative lack of public lavatories in France and the condition of such as existed. She was also scathing about the French diet
of horseflesh, frogs, snails and garlic. The vulgar xenophobic weekly,
John Bull, was written for readers like Mrs Ross. To her, a shop-
keeper in a rather run-down village street which was slowly
degenerating into a thoroughfare in an undistinguished suburb,
Britain had attained a peak of excellence matched by no other
nation. Her worry on behalf of the British Expeditionary Force was
that in order to get at the Germans it had to go to a country so
unworthy of the honour of receiving British troops. She had never
caught up with the *entente cordiale*, and she was uninfluenced by
newspaper pictures of the poilu and Tommy Atkins as comrades in

arms. Not that she was soft towards the Germans. She knew nothing about their public lavatories and did not need to; the Germans were not British and that was sufficient reason for exterminating them. Standing behind her high counter in the steamy shop, raising her voice above the bubbling and hissing, she might have been a robust witch handing out spells instead of large pieces of fried fish for two-pence and a scoopful of chips for a halfpenny.

In normal times the local progressives would have regarded Mrs Ross's political pronouncements with disdain but now (except, per-haps, for reservations in favour of French culture) there could have been little difference between her views and theirs on the war. The heart-searching then going on in Bloomsbury would have found no echo among the local makers of a new world, who accepted that the Kaiser was a monster and the Hun capable of any atrocity. The atti-tude of some sections of the Left, that it was a capitalist war in which the only role of the workers was to overthrow their ex-ploiters, would have seemed incomprehensible to them. Pacifism was utterly alien to even the mildest. One of the politically enlightened teachers taught his class to sing an amended version of Edward German's 'The Yeomen of England' in which the original foemen who cursed the yeomen disappeared and were replaced by 'Austro-Hungarians and German barbarians'. Walter, so prone to lecture con-ferences on the teacher's responsibility for forming the infant mind, was widely quoted by his pupils as having made a joke during a geography lesson on Austria-Hungary; the Austrians, he had pre-dicted, would soon be hungery. Will Crooks, the much-respected Labour Member of Parliament, one of the earliest genuine working-men to be returned to Westminster, spoke for them all at an inter-party recruiting rally at the London Opera House on 11 September, 1914, when he declared that he would 'rather see every living soul blotted off the face of the earth than see the Kaiser supreme any-where'. If the atom bomb had then existed, who can doubt that the politically-advanced workers of the district would have been in favour of using it and proud if they had had a hand in manufactur-ing it?

The comforting belief that the Germans were destined to lose was bolstered by an anecdote about a gypsy's prediction that a war would be lost by a man who mounted his horse from the wrong side. Nobody knew who the gypsy was or where or when this forecast was uttered, but some versions had it that this story had been banned in Germany on the Kaiser's personal orders. No one questioned, either, whether the Kaiser's withered arm compelled him to mount in an unorthodox way. Many of the Estate's residents would have responded somewhat brusquely to a gypsy's offer to tell their fortunes, but an anonymous gypsy was adequate to prophesy the downfall of the German empire.

Angels soon came in on our side. The Angels of Mons myth was said later to have been the unwitting creation of a writer named Arthur Machen, whose imaginative short story about phantom bowmen protecting British soldiers during battle, published in the *Evening News* in September 1914, set off rumours that divine intervention had occurred at critical periods. Anecdotes spread with the rapidity of a virus. Topical artists seized on the theme as a subject for their impressions, depicting giant archers emerging from storm clouds, their bows drawn in the direction of the enemy. Who could query the angels' existence when there were pictures of them in the paper? It required only a slight extension of belief in the angels for people to give credence to reports that German corpses revealed arrow wounds. Belligerent angels inspired school compositions. Teachers raised a laugh by recalling the Kaiser's message to his troops: 'Gott mit uns.' A powerful variant was brought to the Estate by a visiting Anglican clergyman who told it during a Sunday evening sermon.

The setting was just right for a ghost story—the church during the sermon was lit only by candles on the altar, a shaded electric lamp in the pulpit, and a faint glow from the organ loft. The congregation's coughing produced strange echoes, as though a pack of unidentified animals lurked in the gloom. A visiting preacher was always an object of curiosity, and the congregation did not at once compose itself as it did for the vicar's predictable homilies. The opening sentences promised something different. The preacher declared that evidences of a higher world occurred today just as they had two thousand years before. Beings of a superior order still walked the earth and mingled with us. Sometimes, for their own purposes, they revealed themselves for what they were; otherwise they could appear in any guise and any capacity. Occasionally we might suspect that some individual was of a different order from ourselves, or an odd event happened, giving us a hint of a mysterious force at work. We dismissed such revelations because they did not accord with our mundane world. Yet people who had experienced extreme anxiety, found themselves confronted by deadly peril, knew that as the situation grew insupportable aid and comfort came. A close friend of his, whose officer son recently returned to the front after leave in England, had told him this story. (Quoting an impeccable source was, of course, the essential lead-in to this kind of rumour. As the father was a close friend of this clergyman, his credibility was assured. Obviously his son would have been well brought-up and he was now an officer, and thus a responsible person. The incident had actually happened to the son. The implication is that although the account is not first-hand, the witnesses are so reliable that the information is as good as an eye-witness report. Further, it was consistent with other stories, complementing and authenticating them.) During the battle of Mons the son and a fellow officer were riding in darkness along a muddy, shell-torn road. There was a lull in the firing and all they could see in the direction of the front was an occasional star-shell. Exhausted and depressed, they spoke little. Then the son became aware of a third rider. Instead of a companion only on his right side, he also had one on the left. Looking beyond the new-comer, the son perceived yet another rider, and then a long line of mounted men. Awed by the phenomenon, he did not venture to speak but plodded on, glancing when he dared at this mysterious company. He said nothing until they reached a camp, when he realized that the escort had left. Then he learned that his companion had had a similar experience, of being joined first by one silent rider and then by a host. He, too, had been too awed to speak. Both men's hearts were lightened by the thought that they had been under supernatural protection. Why these two had been selected to receive this revelation, and at that particular time, we could not know, but we could be assured that with such forces on our side all would ultimately be well.

Usually the choir adopted the detached pose of semi-professionals to church proceedings. Their uniform of cassock and surplice set them apart from the congregation and put them on the side of the principal performers. They regarded the ranks of worshippers with the amused condescension of those who work behind the scenes. Even the senior choirboy, who was certainly the most pious, had a trick of setting the pitch slightly higher with each succeeding verse of a hymn, so that the congregation were baffled by finding themselves unable to reach the higher notes in the last verse, or he set such a pace for a psalm that the choir finished some bars ahead of everyone else and ostentatiously closed their books while the stragglers were still trying to catch up. On these occasions he was aware that the choir-mistress, who was also the organist, was grimacing into the mirror in which she could see the choir behind and below her, and she expressed her anger by holding on to the opening note of a verse and giving it all the volume she could, or by trying to moderate the speed of a psalm. But he had a loud voice and the choir joyfully followed him, like a pack getting out of hand. He knew that the choir-mistress, formidable character though she was, dared not risk a clash with him. When, in the vestry, she had permitted herself some cross remarks about the choir's indiscipline, he had absented himself from a service at which his singing was particularly required. For the choir to discuss a sermon was not unusual but none had caught their imaginations as had the angelic riders. When they emerged into the street, groups of the congregation still lingered outside, as if expecting that a heavenly host might momentarily be caught in the searchlights. The choir members formed their own group. They had been fascinated not only by the officers' phantom escort but by the assertion that a higher order of beings could be among them, and wondered whether they could identify any. The very few names put forward were unanimously rejected.

No local angels could be detected but it seemed that no one doubted their comforting presence; no one doubted, either, the existence of equally invisible but eerily pervasive spies. From the depths of the woods, so the rumours ran, from the slope near the Peak, from the marshes, spies nightly signalled with flashlamps to one another and to cruising Zeppelins. Some even signalled with matches, a cunning method which enabled any traitor caught in the act to protest that he was only lighting his pipe. Newspapers pointed out that on a clear night the light of a match was visible a mile away—a startling idea for people who could imagine teams of match-striking spies forming a chain of miniature beacons. But the ingenuity of these signallers was outclassed by the agents who transmitted in Morse by manipulating venetian blinds, an operation which would have required quite remarkable dexterity. Many Estate residents must have wondered whether there was any significance in the fact that the gas mantles which illuminated their houses were manufactured by a firm named Welsbach.

Suspicions of agent infiltration, however, were not directed at the Belgian refugees. We learnt of their impending arrival on the day we moved to the new house. Three houses in the next block were being prepared for their reception; it seemed fitting that they should be allotted the most up-to-date accommodation on the Estate. Since the German army invaded 'gallant little Belgium' a David-versus-Goliath stereotype had been imprinted on British minds. A framed reproduction of the violated treaty hung in the school assembly hall beside a portrait of Albert, King of the Belgians. The first 'flag day' that I remember was for Belgian refugees; neat little bows in the Belgian colours, attached to a tiny safety-pin, were sold in the streets. A reception committee was formed (forming committees was one of the major spare-time occupations of Estate residents) and, inevitably, Walter was elected chairman. The co-operative society made the houses available, furnished them and supplied vouchers for free food; the gas company and the water board were, within their own limits, scarcely less generous, and eager well-wishers provided clothing and whatever comforts they thought the victims of Hun frightfulness would need. Schoolchildren were urged to regard the Belgian children as honoured guests. Walter described to his class how Continental roads were lined with fruit trees and asserted that the fruit was never stolen but harvested in an orderly manner; the implication was that children on the Continent were more regardful of communal property than English children were—in similar circumstances—likely to be. The Continent did not, in this context, appear to include Germany and Austria. An impression grew that, as neighbours, the heroic Belgians would take a lot of living up to.

✣ 9 ✣

Dear Old Blighty

People believe rumours and are indignant if anyone tries to refute a widespread story, yet they do not accept the necessary concomitants which would follow if a rumour were a fact. Obviously, if the allegations about the match-strikers and venetian-blind signallers had any substance, an organized network of agents would have been operating on the Estate; at some time they must have been recruited, trained, briefed and installed in their posts; presumably there would have to be liaison with some command post and arrangements to supply funds. The Estate would not have been selected as the sole area of such activity; related networks would have existed throughout the country. With such intensive penetration the enemy must have been well on the way to winning the war. Yet the residents often revealed how little worried they were about the outcome.

Thus, when the *Lusitania* was sunk in May 1915 it was not the submarine blockade which immediately occupied the adults around me; it was how to pronounce the 'a' in the third syllable of the name. The question was answered on the following Sunday, when the vicar prayed for the *Lusitania* victims.

What could have been more indicative of a quiet confidence than the meeting each week of what would now be called a youth group but was then known in this district by the pleasantly evocative name of guild? I relate its proceedings in some detail not only because, locally, it exercised a greater influence on its members than did the school or the church but because, in diverse forms, this type of instruction (propaganda, if you like) was going on all over the country. That it was better organized and more effective on the Estate was due to the presence of two devoted teachers and of numerous parents who approved the guild's purpose. Clean, well turned-out children, polite, compliant and receptive, went through the evening's routine with gusto. Walter and his bouncy wife, Jane, worked hard at providing a social life for the members but their deeper aim was not concealed; it was, in fact, a long-term plan in which the war was an irrelevance.

The programme began with one of the secular hymns which express the Labour movement's emotions. A favourite was 'England arise! The long long night is over, Faint in the East, behold the dawn appear!' The amended 'These things shall be' was Jane's usual choice, and at her request the verse beginning 'They shall be simple in their homes' was sometimes sung twice, because she liked to dwell on the next line: 'And splendid in their public ways.' The God of the non-sectarian progressives was invoked in another: 'When wilt thou save the people, O God of mercy, when? The people, Lord, the people. Not thrones and crowns but men.' More militant was a terrible piece of doggerel sung to the tune of 'Men of Harlech': 'Earnest true co-operation, Be our glorious aspiration, Till we see in every nation, Labour truly free. Hand in hand on pressing, Labour's wrongs redressing, Oh, that we might truly see wide happen many a blessing. . . .'

The lesson was exacting, given by a dedicated man with a serious purpose. Sitting at trestle-tables, the children wrote notes with well-sharpened pencils, aware that an examination would follow at the end of the course. Not three miles away munitions were being turned out on an unprecedented scale; sometimes, faintly but unmistakably, artillery barrages on the western front could be heard on the Estate; a few hundred yards away, on the Peak, the anti-aircraft gun waited with its crew. Inside The Hall the contemporary world was, for the time being, ignored. The Unspeakable Huns, tossing babies on their bayonets, were never mentioned. Nor was this the place for jokes about the Austrians being hungery. An older enemy, of longer standing, was being studied. Walter was teaching industrial history. He spoke eloquently, his expression transformed as though he were seeing visions over our heads. I had a feeling of joining him in the past, of sharing with him a magic lens focused, at first, on the eighteenth century. Today I have only to hear the words 'cottage industry' to be back with him in the yellow gaslight, the fumes of the cast-iron coke-burning stove in my nose, contemplating a textbook picture showing a loom inside a cottage with a view through the open door of a weaver digging his vegetable patch in a rural setting. Of course, Walter emphasized, no one was to harbour an idealized image of England before the 1760s. The weaver and his family worked long hours, they were exploited by the grasping clothiers or intermediaries who handled the product, their lives were frugal; but the inventions which revolutionized industry, caused populations to concentrate near the sources of power, created hells of mean streets and smoke-laden air, still lay in the future. The weaver was not yet a dehumanized factory-hand, cut off from the earth, the fields and hills, a view of the sky. Plants grew for him and the changing seasons provided pleasures later unknown to dwellers in the squalid alleys and courtyards of northern industrial towns in the early nineteenth century. Although the cottage worker might start weaving as soon as light permitted, he saw the splendour of the dawn and felt the fresh morning breeze on his face. The children worked too and were uneducated, yet they knew the simple joy of wandering through fields—another picture showed sun-bonneted little girls making daisy-chains.

Then came the inventors—Richard Trevithick, James Watt, Richard Arkwright, Samuel Crompton, James Hargreaves—whose inventions should have lightened man's lot. The ethic of the time did not point in that direction. Sombrely Walter dwelt on Adam Smith, Malthus, factory owners' opposition to government regulation, the evidence given to government commissions. The movement of population to the new industrial centres took those little girls from sunlit fields to dark slums.

As they were southerners, nearly all of them born on the Estate, his students did not know the Lancashire towns described so movingly by Walter and the textbook-writers. My ideas of them formed a collage, foreshortened in time, with the overall impression of an inferno. The picture comes back vividly; it is ineradicable. In the small hours, in an imagined town, only the mill is alive with light and pulsing machines. Through the frosty streets shuffles the yawning knocker-up, holding a pole with which he rattles a bunch of keys against upper windows. Grey-faced weary people groan, crawl from under rags, shake children. Suddenly the town wakes to the sound of clogs, coughing, and crying babies; haggard men lurch through the gloom; women carry still-sleeping toddlers wrapped in their shawls. Undernourished and underclad orphans, their teeth chattering from the cold, their eyes wide with fear, are hustled along by the shouts and blows of brutal overseers. Through all the hours of daylight, until after night has fallen again, these slaves—many misshapen by their work or through accidents or disease—will tend machines. Toddlers, at the risk of being maimed or killed, crawl under looms to remove fluff. Boy chimney-sweepers, their knees and elbows raw, are climbing chimneys; when they get caught in the bends, fires are lit below to force them to struggle free. Below ground, sweating miners are hacking at coal, sometimes in workings so narrow that they cannot turn round. Nearly naked women, harnessed like animals, are pulling laden coal-trucks. These victims are cheated by the truck system and combinations of workmen are illegal. Most are property-less, ignorant and defenceless, buying oblivion in gin (Walter's usually equable manner faltered as he quoted 'drunk for a penny, dead drunk for twopence'), or expressing their rage in senseless outbursts of violence which are ruthlessly put down by the militia.

The industrial revolution, which could have produced immeasurable benefits, had unleashed an evil force to blacken the skies, disfigure the landscape, pollute the rivers and poison men's hearts. Instead of the profits accruing to the community, they had gone to private individuals whose ruthlessness in competing with one another had excluded all compassion and even the most elementary consideration for their fellow men. All society's ills were diagnosed as resulting from competition in the search for private profit. At the foot of the weekly cyclostyled lesson notes there appeared, in Jane's firm round hand: 'Co-operation is life! Competition is death.' The quotation was from Ruskin, but it was never attributed to a mortal source; it was inspired basic truth, to be illustrated but not debated.

Great and good men had appeared—the Earl of Shaftesbury, who championed factory-workers, and the Christian Socialists. Greatest of all was Robert Owen (the Estate's unofficial patron saint) who had preached the new moral world. Workers had combined in trade unions. Co-operative societies, eliminating private profit and its attendant evils, had spread throughout the country; like the municipal trams, they merited support for moral reasons. The Estate was a co-operative colony, part of a process which eventually would develop into the Co-operative Commonwealth.

In the meantime the students had to learn to conduct a business meeting. Following the lecture, Walter abdicated his leading role in favour of an elected youthful chairman who took his (or her) place at a table with the secretary, treasurer and committee members. The chairman declared the meeting open, read the agenda and 'called upon' the secretary to read the minutes of the previous meeting. Members moved and seconded the adoption of the minutes, the chairman took a vote, and then asked: 'Are there any questions arising from the minutes?' To an outsider it might have seemed a piece of childish play-acting, an inflated procedure for dealing with such matters as a Christmas dance; but it was the drill rather than the subject matter which was important. Members, and especially chairmen, learnt to ensure that motions were properly moved; they knew that an amendment when carried becomes the substantive motion; they learnt to crush the pest, present at every meeting, who tries to put points of order which are not points of order. Since then I have wondered why hardly any adult chairmen know the rules as those children did; I have squirmed at the tangle which highly-paid officials make of straightforward discussions, and sympathized with despairing secretaries trying to sort out, after the chairman and his cronies have moved to the bar, what the meeting has decided, if anything. The guild's records were always clear, its accounts exact. The chairman formally declared the meeting closed.

A curious interval of uproar then occurred. The guild members, for the past hour so docile, sprang to their feet, hurled their chairs to the sides of the room, violently dismantled the trestle-tables, all the time shouting, screaming and laughing, grappling wildly with each other. Walter, experienced in controlling children, ignored them. In three or four minutes, as suddenly as it had started, the clamour ceased. No one had given a sign or uttered an admonition. It was, perhaps, a childish, brief version of *Fasching*; regularly, at stated intervals, the respectable, industrious and rather repressed community indulges in a hilarious outburst of unconventional behaviour, yet adheres to a convention that normal behaviour is abruptly restored when the period of licence is over.

The final hour of games and dancing was decorously jolly. Musical chairs and spinning the plate were played with intense attention. Jane enjoyed vigorous square-dances like Sir Roger de Coverley and The Lancers; untiringly she pushed and pulled groups through the figures. Here again, as in the business meeting, the proper order was rigidly observed. If a single child made a false opening step, everybody was stopped and told to start again. None of this discipline occasioned the slightest resentment; children accepted that there was a right and a wrong way of doing things and they expected to be corrected if they made mistakes.

Walter's formula for closing the evening—'Get your cloaks and bonnets!'—always raised a good-humoured laugh because of its quaintness. He stood at the door, slowing up the departing children so that they should not crowd through it and fall down the stone steps outside, and he urged them to go home quietly so that 'our neighbours' should not be disturbed by noise. Thus conditioning in social behaviour went on to the last moment. In a few minutes all the children were home, being served with cocoa or Horlicks and biscuits by parents who were unceasingly anxious about their off-spring's nourishment.

While the Belgians were being awaited, another invasion began. No committee was formed to welcome these new arrivals; school-children were not urged to treat them as guests; Walter did not cite them as models of behaviour. The violation of the Estate began with the marking-out of an area hitherto reserved for brick owner-occupied houses and temporarily devoted to allotments. Huge quantities of planks, asbestos and roofing material were deposited on this site. Hutments, as they were called, were to be erected for munitions workers and their families from distant industrial districts. 'An eye-sore' was the immediate judgement of Estate residents who, obsessed by the permanence of bricks and mortar, predicted that in no time these sheds (as critics called them) would become a scene of squalor and dilapidation. A deeper emotion also underlay the residents' re-action. Many of the newcomers were unskilled or semi-skilled men. They were the harbingers of 'dilution'—the introduction into fac-tories of a much higher proportion of non-craftsmen than had hither-to been the custom. Those skilled men who saw dilution as a per-manent encroachment on their status were right.

The hutments, precursors of the Second World War prefabs, were individually and stoutly built by carpenters and joiners, who measured, cut and fitted the wood on the site. The dwellings looked, not unpleasingly, like a child's early drawings of a house: rectan-gular, with sloping roofs, a front door in the middle and a square four-paned window on either side of it. They were, for the period, quite well-equipped, and evoked from Estate residents who were invited to inspect them such patronizing remarks as: 'They'll be better than the poor things are used to.' The prediction was true; war raises many people's living standards, and for the first time these newcomers had space round them and regular money to spend. Some soon made their gardens look like a second-hand dealer's yard; others produced displays which Estate gardeners stopped to admire; but, however they varied, they were given a collective character as 'hut dwellers'. An invisible frontier existed between the two com-munities.

A very different reception awaited the representatives of gallant little Belgium. An appeal was made for French speakers; the result would certainly not have been overwhelming. But the reception committee would have been untrue to the nature of committees if speeches had not been made, refreshment provided, and a helpful escort formed to take them to the houses which were to be their refuge. Their arrival was awaited with intense curiosity; foreigners were as rare in the neighbourhood as countesses. Everybody had watched with pride the furniture, carpets, curtains, gas ovens, bathroom geysers, bed linen, cushions, crockery, flour-bins, bread-pans and garden tools being delivered. Nothing had been forgotten. The Estate was paying its tribute to the little army which had held up the German advance. Everyone was ready to smile and wave.

Any smiles the Belgians may have encountered surely soon changed to expressions of incredulity. A curious contingent, supposedly consisting of three families, had moved in. If the puzzled committee got them sorted out, the neighbours never decided with certainty who the large shrill woman was, which slattern was married to which man, who were the parents of the children. Perhaps the men caused the greatest surprise because they were excessively unmilitary in their cloth caps, jerseys, workmen's trousers and plimsolls (worn, it was conjectured, to give them speed in getting away). Soon it became apparent that they were more than three families and not on the best of terms with each other; the decorum of the district was shattered by the sound of their disputes. The younger ones startled the repressed local children by their boisterousness and evident mania for destruction. Perhaps it was because of the parents' idea to keep the children occupied that a large couch, the gift of some local philanthropist, was dragged into the garden, where it was speedily dismantled and the débris hurled over the fences of garden-proud neighbours. If these were the children who never plundered roadside fruit trees, they had decided that different conventions prevailed in England. They chased each other into neighbours' front gardens, a trespass no Estate child would have committed. They flung waste paper, straw from packing-cases and broken crockery into the street. The small front gardens, neatly planted before their arrival, were turned into junk heaps. New, strongly-built dustbins were battered out of shape, a process which caused loud noises over a long period. Glaziers made not infrequent calls to mend broken windows. The gas-meter reader described a hole hacked in the party wall between two of the houses, and a devastated living-room. The men, who for a long time had no employment, got help-lessly drunk in the local pubs and were gently helped home by tolerant police; embarrassed committee members—some of them tee-totallers—explained that the guests were unaccustomed to the strength of English beer. But what occasioned the greatest outrage was their reckless ordering of food from the stores. The panic which had emptied the shelves at the start of the war had not recurred and a kind of unofficial rationing had come into operation. Patient cus-tomers, waiting to buy a small allocation of sugar, tea, bacon or butter, watched while the large shrill Belgian woman, attended by compatriots who would help to carry the goods, pointed imperiously in this direction and that and paid no money.

With the stories of German frightfulness in mind, and impressed by the Belgian resistance, people put up with a lot before expressing dis-approval of the representatives of our gallant ally. No such inhibi-tions were felt by a fellow Belgian refugee, a dapper little man who, apparently sponsored by no organization, arrived on his own, found and paid for his lodging, and worked on the night shift in a muni-tions factory. He would have nothing to do with these problem families and he declared that they ought to be made to work and keep themselves; so long as they were given something for nothing, he said, they would accept it and make no effort. His views were repeated by his landlady with a certain awe and relayed among the suffering neighbours. He was not, of course, the only self-supporting refugee; others, including some admirable young women school-teachers, lived quietly and worked hard. They were scarcely noticed; local attention was focused on their compatriots who were seizing the opportunity to live a life of Saturday nights. The committee had had a rough bunch foisted on them. As householders, schooled in prudent housekeeping and orderliness, conscious of having paid for everything they owned, they were bewildered and dismayed by casual destruction. They remained discreet, and it was not until years later that Walter, with characteristic mildness, admitted that the committee's work 'was not of the easiest'.

If they had shared Mrs Ross's view that all foreigners were un-desirable and must be handled with firmness and caution, they would probably have coped better. Her opinion of aliens would have corres-ponded broadly with the local attitude to the shiftless British poor. Had the unlikely proposal been made that the occupants of the nearby slum should be rescued from their squalor, lodged in respectable new houses without charge, given free clothing, handed vouchers exchangeable for any food they fancied, and provided with pocket money to spend as they liked, even the most naively charitable would have declared such generosity misplaced. They might not actually have used that phrase about coals in the bath, but they would have meant something very like it. Certainly they would have foreseen the noise, the destruction and the drunkenness, and had a rescue operation none the less been put into effect it would have been conducted on a realistic basis of punishments and rewards.

The trams now came into their own. Walter and the pro-tram pressure group ought, after the war, to have received a share of the O.B.E.s which were scattered, like carnival confetti, on the multitude. Had they lived on the level at which people write their memoirs, they would have claimed that they foresaw the necessity of establishing a transport network capable of carrying the unceasing flow of munitions workers from a wide area to a concentration of factories during the inevitable and imminent war. The fact that they had not publicly mentioned their motives at the time could have been explained by their reluctance to alarm the public. The tracks were there, the tram is simple to build, and almost overnight the fleet was so expanded that Walter could seldom have left his house without seeing a tram, and it would have been nothing unusual if he had seen four or five. Despite occasional hold-ups, when a tram was derailed or a trolley-pole jumped the overhead wire and the rope swung tantalizingly just out of the conductor's reach, the London area has never had such a cheap, frequent and reliable public transport system.

Walter claimed no credit for his foresight but he not infrequently reminded his guild members and school pupils of their moral duty, when in an area where alternative transport systems were available, to give preference to the publicly-owned one. Responsive though I was to his ideology, I had reservations about trams, not only because they made children sick, but because I had observed that the crews held a contrary ideology. While passengers were endeavouring to use the trams which they, in theory, owned, the tram crews were determined to prevent them doing so whenever they saw the chance. I often witnessed occasions when tram crews nearly achieved their ideal of a tram with no passengers.

A passenger would know that 'operation passenger-dodging' was on if he happened to be on an almost empty tram a few minutes before it was due to pass the Ordnance-factory gates when a shift was due out. The conductor would look at his watch and then go forward to the driver's platform, where there would be a short discussion. Then the tram shot forward—the acceleration was very good—and the conductor lurched back to his place at the rear to repel would-be boarders if the vehicle had to slow down. Rocking alarmingly, the wheels roaring, the driver's bell clanging continuously, the tram hurtled past stops. Waiting would-be passengers were ignored, their beseeching looks, gesticulations and sometimes shouts attracting only contemptuous glances. Passengers already on the tram, and who wanted to alight, had to ring the bell repeatedly and outface the conductor's hostility. The crew's tactic then was to drive past the stop, to avoid the danger that waiting persons might be so presumptuous as to try to get on, and to halt between stops, where nobody would be waiting. It did not take long, if the tram had a clear run, before a tram ahead was sighted. Probably the crew of this one too were alert to the danger that they might soon be required to pick up a lot of tired workers. If they were not, the driver of the second tram shouted a warning to the conductor of the first, and he promptly took action by signalling on his bell to his driver. This procedure could result in a convoy of perhaps seven trams, with an overall carrying capacity of a thousand passengers, racing along the roads like a presidential escort. For such passengers as were already on board and booked to the terminus it was an exhilarating experience. When the tram was clear of the factory gates self-congratulations were bawled between the two crew members, and these were never so loud as when it was seen that they had only just made it, that the following driver had been compelled to stop by an advance party of emerging workers who—familiar with these daily manœuvres—rushed straight out of the gates and on to the tram track. Then the *Schadenfreude* of the tram men who had won this game by such a narrow margin could not be contained. At the terminus, in great good humour, they left their vehicle at the tail of the long queue of trams which had been so speedily brought out of the danger zone, and waited in a boisterous group to shout friendly insults at the next arrivals who had just endured three miles of stopping, starting and collecting fares.

Munitions workers did not constitute the only crowds they tried to avoid; they were fully alert to the unreasonable demands made on them by cinema-goers, weekend shoppers, schoolchildren and people turned out of pubs at closing time. But to none of these groups did they show the same united front as they did to the men and women who were, in the phrase of the time, feeding the guns. What the tram men resented was that the munitions workers were drawing big wages. With the press, and apparently a large section of society excepting shopkeepers and publicans, they appeared to hold the view that the order of things was outraged if factory workers (and miners, who were victims of the same resentment) earned wages which went above an accustomed level. Before the war a highly-skilled man on the Estate thought himself not badly-off on £2 a week, and he would have known plenty of men who received little more than half that. When, at the beginning of the war, they started to work twelve-hour shifts, with one day off once a fortnight, they were paid proportionately higher wages. Instead of this increase seeming to be an obvious consequence, it aroused astonishment and indignation.

Far from 'Hand in hand on pressing, Labour's wrongs redressing', the workers were glancing sideways at each other, envious and protesting if one group appeared to forge ahead faster than their own. Theirs was a static view of society. Each group had its allotted place and, by implication, would be unhappy or ridiculous if the order were changed. I did not hear the apocryphal anecdotes about miners from the reactionary bourgeoisie; they were circulating among people who were proud to call themselves working class. One story, as told in the South, concerned a miner; probably, in other areas, the central character was a munitions worker. The miner was said to have entered a shop and paid cash for a piano. Soon after, he returned and bought another, paying for that with cash too and remarking that the first piano looked so nice on one side of the room that he wished to match it with one on the other side. Possibly this story had its origin in snobbish cartoons; it bears a resemblance to *Punch* jokes about the *nouveau riche* who acquired possessions—a grand piano, pictures, antiques, a cellar—which under some natural law he was not entitled to have and who presumed to pursue activities such as hunting, shooting, golf, dining in smart restaurants and going to the opera which, lacking as he did an inborn expertise and style, made him look ridiculous. Whatever the source of the story about the miner's piano, it was repeated as true and as though it proved something.

Even more malicious stories were told about women munitions workers. Craftsmen were prejudiced against them because of the dreaded dilution; unskilled men because female labour spared them for military service; housewives because they thought other women ought not to have so much money. They were fast hussies, squandering their wages on paint and powder, drenched in cheap scent, loaded with trashy jewellery, wearing (the traditional rewards for less arduous services) silk stockings and fur coats. The highest paid worked in a T.N.T. filling factory; their faces and hands were yellow and so were the wisps of hair escaping from under their caps. In keeping with the air of jollity which characterized the time, they were popularly known as 'canaries'. The noxious substance which dyed their skins was also absorbed by their lungs and stomachs; perhaps, coming from forebears who had spent their working lives breathing industrial fumes and dust, they stoically accepted that the money earned in youth had to be repaid by a premature death or by years of infirmity. Their apparently unceasing hilarity may have been their way of repressing thoughts of their fate. They were in the Phil May tradition, boisterous, coarse and assertive, but their riotous behaviour was always kept within limits, as when they linked arms, spread themselves across the roadway, and strode along singing and shouting. Tram-drivers, slowed down to walking pace, stamped repeatedly on their bells; lorry-drivers hooted and shouted—the din implied less annoyance than participation in the fun. Suddenly, before the obstruction became serious, the line of girls broke in the middle; half swung to one side of the road and half to the other, and they laughed and waved as the traffic moved again.

Other evidences of prosperity escaped censure. Children acquired bicycles, scooters, watches with luminous dials, and khaki handkerchiefs. Music teachers flourished. George Robey and Violet Lorraine singing 'If you were the only girl in the world' could be heard on horn gramophones in numerous front rooms. The gramophone, however, did not rival the piano as a status symbol; no stories circulated about affluent workers buying two gramophones.

It took people some time to grasp that jobs could be had by anybody. When a local Army Pay Corps office engaged fourteen-year-old girls straight from school at fifteen shillings a week the lavishness of this pay even caused some disquiet; my paternal grandfather, conditioned to the idea of seven-year apprenticeships, wondered whether it was 'good' for untrained girls to earn so much money.

Young married women appeared behind the grocery and provision counters at the stores and were immediately judged as less capable than the men, no allowance being made for the men's years of carving, slicing, weighing and packing. It must have been nerve-racking for a woman, before all those hard eyes and pressed lips, to try to emulate the men who could pat butter, or cut cheese with a wire, then toss the portion on to the scales and know precisely what it would weigh.

The conduct of the war did not appear to require the cancellation of school holidays in 1915 and the subsequent years so we were able to resume our annual three weeks at the seaside. Margate being subject to the danger of air raids and naval bombardment, we went to Bognor or Eastbourne. These excursions were less leisurely. The trunk and the wicker basket no longer stood open for weeks before our departure. My father could not accompany us, and we struggled desperately with suitcases on to overcrowded trains which ran late. We spent the journey in a state of anxiety, heightened when the train stood for long periods between stations and passengers speculated on the reasons. The holiday did not begin until we saw the waiting line of landaus at the station, and the familiar thrill returned when the driver waved his whip and the horse started to trot.

The system had not changed since before the war. We rented apartments, my mother bought the food, and the landlady prepared the meals. She also became temporarily a confidante of my mother, told us how she had lost her husband (the landladies were all widows) and related the origins of the various pieces of furniture, a recital which involved the production of the family portrait album so that we could see the features of the person who had bequeathed the article under discussion. The great event in one woman's life had been her move from Weymouth to Bognor. She habitually conversed via her cat—'You came from Weymouth in a basket, didn't you, Billy?' was the introductory sentence. She treated us with a consideration due to refugees from a war zone and frequently remarked, as she asked for first-hand accounts of air raids: 'We think they're very brave to go on living there, don't we, Billy?'

South-coast towns seemed quiet compared with bustling pre-war Margate. Camouflaged shipping convoys, painted so that they looked out of the water, passed on the horizon, and small airships known as blimps patrolled the Channel. Occasionally on the wind came the faint rumble of gunfire. My mother, fully clothed and wearing a hat, sat on the beach under a sunshade, brooding about rising prices, insolent tradespeople, and my father's safety. She imagined herself opening the door to a policeman's knock, listening to his attempt to break the news gently—the ordeal undergone by a neighbour whose husband, after years of inspecting hand grenades, was blown to pieces by a faulty one. Her friend Mrs Humbert, mother of the young man with the correct Teutonic manners, had also been widowed; her husband, after being struck on the head by a piece of moving machinery, had refused treatment, gone home at the usual time and fallen into a coma.

The Regimental Sergeant Major was dead, victim of a drama played out in the secret military world in which he had spent his life. A young lieutenant had brought a charge against him. Mrs Empson never learnt what the trouble was about; probably, as an army wife inhibited by years of protocol, she did not press very hard. The court dismissed the charge, and hundreds of men cheered him as he emerged with his honourable record unblemished. He walked straight to his quarter, and a few minutes later shot himself.

For a brief while young Mr Fish occupied public attention. Anxious to get into the war before it ended, he had the good luck— I am using the vocabulary of the time—to be accepted. He was 'fortunate enough' (I remember reading the expression in a magazine) to be sent on active service. After a few months in France he had another kind of luck; he 'got a Blighty one'. Hundreds of people, waving handkerchiefs and tiny Union Jacks, waited outside the church to see him, now without the left arm and the right leg, emerge with his bride, amid clouds of confetti, and drive away in a white wedding-carriage drawn by two ribbon-bedecked greys. It was a rare scene of jubilation.

❧ 10 ❧

A Single Cheer

When the milkman changed a pound note for my mother, he begged her not to tell anybody. Paper money, as a replacement for the golden sovereign, was regarded with distrust. Sharply rising prices aroused incredulity; in people's minds, the proper prices for a loaf, a quart of milk, a pint of beer, a peck of potatoes, were those obtaining before the war. Still greater astonishment occurred when workers discovered that they were liable to income tax—hitherto thought to be a just tax designed to relieve the wealthy of part of their un-deserved riches; to workers who had previously kept all their wages, it seemed that the government was practising a fraud by pretending to pay them a specific amount when it was in fact paying them a lesser sum. Adjustment to such now-familiar features of life did not come easily.

The breaking of the fourth Commandment was not lightly accep-ted. Munitions workers could not be held responsible for Sunday shifts, but that, as Mrs Perry and other religious wives at first argued, did not absolve them from Sabbath observance when they had the day free. No doubt they feared that one relaxation would lead to others, and their forebodings were quickly confirmed. Soon men in old clothes could be seen in their gardens and allotments on Sunday mornings, regardless of whether church-goers passed by. Sabbatarians had to ask themselves whether God preferred them to wait, possibly for an hour, in a potato queue, go without potatoes, or agree that their husbands should plant potatoes on a Sunday. Mostly they decided that God was, in the circumstances, likely to be as liberal about vegetable cultivation as he was over munitions manufacture. They could still give rulings on such indulgences as bicycle-riding, card and dice games, and any music on Sunday except hymns and the dullest piano exercises but, none the less, female power had been eroded.

With increasing fatigue my father's eccentricities became more marked. When he should have been sleeping he would get out of bed to check the gas and water taps, and he 'worked himself up', as my mother put it, over what he regarded as official idiocies. A

poster reading EAT LESS BREAD aroused his scorn. Less than
how much? he would ask. What should one eat instead? In the
absence of an alternative, the poster's real meaning was EAT LESS.
Follow that advice and you would soon be told that you needed less
money to live on. Yet he was not a nervous man; in danger he became detached. He was in a workshop, among explosives, when fire
broke out. Shortly after he got outside, the place blew up, and he
was interested to observe that the building behaved as it was supposed
to. The roof came off and the walls held. His admiring comment was
that the men who had designed it knew their job; it was the highest
praise he could give. The incident seemed to cheer him up.

He shared the skilled men's misgivings about dilution, but he
liked the variety of men it brought into the workshop. During the
night-shift meal-break, impromptu concerts were held. One of the
temporary machine-hands was a cellist; his playing, especially
because it was in that unlikely setting, gave my father enormous
pleasure—the floor vibrated to that wonderful sound, he said. A
music-hall comedian sang 'I'm Major General Worthington' (a number the audience never tired of because of its cynicism) and solos
from Gilbert and Sullivan operas. At other times, while eating his
sandwiches and drinking dry ginger ale—he disapproved of men who
brought beer—he enjoyed talking to a clergyman, and he was upset
when the young man was killed riding home on a motor-cycle. He
was sorry for the family men who had rushed into munitions to
avoid the Army, and who were bound, eventually, to be flushed out
and have their places taken by women.

Men who tried to find jobs which would keep them out of the
Army were described in newspapers as searching for 'a funk hole'.
According to the recruiting poster, the women of England said 'Go'.
The refrain of a popular song was: 'We don't want to lose you but
we think you ought to go.' Such sentiments were not widespread on
the Estate. Young Mr Fish was admired but not regarded as an
example to be emulated. Mr Wyatt (Jim, who had soft hands) was
generally congratulated when he found the finest funk hole of all—
in Washington. His family could not accompany him, but they were
to receive what seemed to them a handsome allowance and they
were comforted by the thought that he would be three thousand
miles away from the trenches.

Horatio Bottomley failed to persuade the country to adopt the
comic-paper expression Germ-huns, and there was amusement in the

stores when German sausage was renamed breakfast sausage. But witch-hunters emerged. One Saturday morning word spread through the Estate that a crowd was assembling in the village. When people stand still and stare, others join them to find out the cause. Tramwaymen at the terminus stood in a cluster at one end of the street, speculating on what was happening; at the other end were the station-master, and the boy scouts who, unable to plead any longer the military necessity of guarding the railway bridge, had taken to hanging about it on Saturdays, chasing up and down the steps and standing in the smoke and steam of engines passing underneath. The crowd grew until it blocked the street.

Inside her shop Mrs Ross was frying the fish and chips which would constitute the midday meal of many local families; the waiting customers, enjoying the aroma, were asking each other what so many people were expecting. Absorbed in her work, she remarked that the crowd had been there for some while but she had been too busy to find out why. Slowly came the realization that the people nearest the fish shop were the nucleus of the crowd; they were facing its steamy windows and peering in. A customer went outside and was seen to be talking to a youth. Through the open door words and phrases drifted in above the hissing of the hot fat. The woman who had gone out was protesting. The youth's voice was high-pitched, hysterically accusing. Mr Ross, he said, was a German; before the war he had changed his name. Customers gasped at the idea that Mrs Ross, the arch-patriot, the personification of the insular, blindly loyal, xenophobic Briton, should ever have consented to marry a German. Conversation ceased and they stared at her.

She turned her back and seemed absorbed in prodding the fish under the bubbling fat. Then suddenly she straightened, turned, flung up the flap at the end of the counter, pushed past her customers, and took up a position just in front of her doorway. That familiar voice, raised now to carry the length of the street, which had for years proclaimed Britain's unassailable greatness and the inferiority in every respect of other nations, ordered the crowd to clear off. Faced with this enraged fishwife, this working-class Britannia, the front rows fell back. The demonstrators were irresolute and no one gave a lead. The crowd behind started to disperse; possibly some of them realized that to be identified by Mrs Ross would mark them down for some formidable abuse in future. Silently, having assured herself that everybody was on the move, she came back into

E   [129]

the shop and recommenced serving. Nobody dared to ask her about the incident. She and her husband (who, if he was a German, showed remarkable acting ability in impersonating a Kentish fishmonger) remained unmolested for the duration of the war, he to collect crates of fish from the station, she to serve customers and to provide war commentaries in which British set-backs were minimized, the French and the Russians berated for their bungling, the United States sharply observed, and all Germans, Austrians and Turks condemned to extinction.

A couple of miles away a mob met no resistance when, early one morning, they attacked a baker's shop owned by a real German. He had worked in England for thirty years and had never bothered about naturalization; before 1914 people came and went without passports and they needed no work permits. Bakers were local personalities, as identified with the quality and taste of their bread as vintners with their wine. They did not need to delude their customers into believing that their product was baked in a farm kitchen or remind them that wheat was ripened by the sun. Loaves came into the shop warm from the bakehouse. This man's reputation did not save him. A crowd smashed his shop windows, wrecked his fittings and threw loaves into the roadway. A light rain was falling and it was a dismal sight, from a passing tram, to see bread trampled under horses' hooves, pulped in the tram lines and merged into the mud. The attack must have caused considerable noise but no one intervened and nobody was ever arrested for what was, at a time when British food ships were being sunk by enemy submarines, a serious act of sabotage. On occasions the police can be remarkably shy. After the damage was done a single policeman stood with his back to the gaping shop, until the windows were boarded up and the business closed down. Although nothing could compensate the baker for this outrage, he was at least spared having to bake the standard bread which, later in the war, was not only unpalatable but was suspected of causing rashes.

Irrational anger ought to have been appeased by the sight of burning Zeppelins; surely one can have no greater revenge than to see one's enemy consumed by flames. Our anxiety, during the raids, was that we should not miss seeing the Zeppelin in the searchlights after the exciting preliminaries of getting up, drinking tea and eating biscuits at an unaccustomed hour, and hearing the approaching gunfire. We had grown used to the spectacle of an airship's passing on the way to London and then its return; it looked serenely remote and apparently immune to the shells bursting around it. One night in September 1916 we were, in effect, watching a Zeppelin go by, expecting to see it disappear out of the range of the local searchlights and guns, when a glowing red spot appeared on the underside. A voice in the neighbourhood said it was a signal—not an improbable suggestion granted the presumption that along its route agents were lighting matches and signalling with venetian blinds. But this idea could be entertained only for a few seconds. The light rapidly spread along the length of the aircraft, and then flames became visible. A vast glow was diffused over the sky, while the Zeppelin seemed to hang motionless. Seconds later it began slowly to break up, but before then a tremendous noise of applause, led by ships' sirens and train whistles, sounded. The trams, stopped during the alert, had stood dark and silent, spaced out on the track; now the drivers jumped repeatedly on their bells and shouted in frenzy. Windows and doors were flung open, and laughter was heard all round, while sections of the disintegrating craft, blazing fiercely, floated downwards. New Year's Eve never produced such a clamour. Guy Fawkes night bonfires never lit up excited faces so vividly. Surely at no time in history had men been done to death amid the ecstatic jubilation of such a huge audience. For once the population had seen an indisputable victory after two years of waiting to move the flags eastward on the maps and to learn that the cavalry had gone through. Before their eyes the enemy had attacked and been annihilated. Some people did not go back to bed at all that night. A month later the scene was repeated. This time we were waiting to see the Zeppelin shot down. The din, mechanical and human, was tremendous. My mother wondered whether there had been time for the crew to hear it before they died.

Although no policemen appeared when Mrs Ross's shop was threatened, and they apparently heard no sound while the mob attacked the bakery, they dealt expeditiously with a more conventional offender who could claim no patriotic motives. The original Estate residents were as law-abiding as any community could well be; such trouble as the local police had came from alien elements— the riotous Belgians and the imported soldiers and munitions workers. The first delinquent on the Estate caused such horror that he was for years mentioned in conversation as though he were the archetypal criminal. He was Hubert, the quietly-spoken young man who had acquired his formal manners in Germany, whose father had not long before died following an industrial accident. The shock was the greater because the local married women regarded him as the model son. He had qualified at his trade, which achievement called for some years of steady application, he was well-spoken and carefully turned out. As he left for the factory, he might have been a young professional man going to an office.

When a policeman called on his mother her first thought was that he had had an accident; as nobody had telephones, the police were the bringers of bad news. The policeman would have known the character of the Estate and realized the effect of his news on such a household; Mrs Humbert related that he had tried to break the news gently and had been sympathetic. But no sympathetic words could diminish the fact that Hubert was under arrest and would appear in court the following morning. It was an era when respectable people never doubted the rightness of the police and the courts; even to be arrested, to have given grounds for suspicion, was a disgrace.

The case turned out to be much worse than she had anticipated. Her son had stolen a bicycle, an easy enough crime to commit as hundreds were parked in the factory yard. All he needed to do was to choose one belonging to a man on a different shift. Then he rode it to a London suburb, about eight miles away. At this apparently safe distance he offered it for sale to a cycle dealer. A brief conversation caused the dealer to think that Hubert, respectable though he seemed, was not as familiar with the machine as an owner might be expected to be. He proposed an arrangement which would have alerted a more experienced crook to danger; he agreed to Hubert's price but pleaded that he had no spare cash in the shop. Hubert was to call again in a few days' time. Meanwhile he passed the details of the machine to the police whose diminished staff could, even during the war, take the trouble to check the description with that of bicycles reported missing over a wide area. When Hubert appeared to claim the money he was kept waiting, still unsuspecting, until a policeman arrived. It was a fair cop but Hubert did not have the sense to go quietly. Surprisingly for a lightweight unaccustomed to brawls, he put up such a fight that reinforcements were needed to subdue him. What then happened was a nasty revelation to Hubert, although it would have caused no astonishment to anyone lower down the social scale. Without waiting for justice to be formally done by the magistrate, the police set to work on him in a way calculated to ensure that in the future he would fear, if not respect, a blue uniform. In court a police witness explained that the prisoner's battered appearance was the consequence of the force necessary to get him to the station. Before Hubert was sentenced to three months his mother, watching the proceedings through her black veil, had another shock. If she had ever been in a court before she would have guessed what was going to happen when a police inspector stepped forward holding a paper. Up to that moment she had had no inkling of her son's previous conviction—a fine for stealing tools.

It is no dramatic exaggeration to say that she never wholly recovered from this experience. She took him back on the morning when, his sentence served, he hid behind a wall until the road seemed empty and then—his coat collar up and his face in a handkerchief—he ran to her front door. She spoke about him to her closest friends, but always in terms of her awed bewilderment. She would not have dissented from local public opinion, which simply condemned Hubert as a bad man. No one—not even the most progressive—defended him on the grounds that his parents had erred in his upbringing, that there were inadequate facilities in the locality for playing games, that there were no outlets for an adventurous spirit, that the Estate had no cinema, or that he was depressed by his father's death or the mass slaughter across the Channel. Just as an advancing army does not stop to repair a broken-down vehicle but simply pushes it off the road, so an advancing class jostled Hubert aside as a non-runner.

With the demise of the Zeppelins (celebrated—a sign of what was happening to popular music—in a parody, sung by children in the streets, of 'Back Home in Tennessee': 'Back home in Germany, That Zepp will never be') my sense of participation in the war faded. The Zeppelin had something of the majesty of a battleship and at the same time a suggestion of the grotesque, as though, in its wartime role, it had been devised by the mad scientists who figured so frequently in boys' adventure stories. Later raids, carried out by aeroplanes which newspapers identified as Gothas, were brief and provided little spectacle, except for one occasion when a substantial number flew in daylight over London in an apparently leisurely fashion.

At school, substitute teachers appeared and took over subjects at some unfamiliar point in the syllabus, threw their classes into almost hysterical confusion and then disappeared. The flags on the maps were ignored and the war was presented as a succession of gallant deeds by heroes on our side: a midshipman stayed at his post while his ship sank, a single soldier annihilated a machine-gun crew who were holding up a British advance, a motor-cycle dispatch rider dashed along a road raked by enemy fire; and cowardly acts by the other side: shelling towns occupied by civilians, bombing Red Cross transports and sinking merchant ships. The names of our heroes would live for ever more; the Huns' crimes would never be forgotten or forgiven.

The assurance that Kitchener had not perished with the *Hampshire* was relayed by Mrs Empson, who had startled my mother—slow to grasp that not only girls but women of almost any age could get a job—by going to work in an army records office, as much for the company as the money. 'We have many a good laugh,' she said. One cause of mirth, I gathered from her anecdotes about the office, was the word posterior on a form containing details of wounds. The office was also a clearing house for rumours about preparations for decisive offensives, the opening of new fronts, the state of German supplies (they were cooking rats and washing with soap made from corpses). Kitchener's survival had been unmistakably hinted at in letters from prisoners of war, in which the writers used such guarded phrases as 'You'd be surprised to know who's with us here!' A curious minor rumour concerned luminous watch dials, then a novelty; nervous people, waking in a drowsy state in a dark room and forgetting the existence of the watch, were said to have been terrified by the glowing points of light and to have aroused the household by screams.

The war years brought the completion of a change in the routine of family life which had begun before 1914. The first films I saw, before any cinemas had been built, were shown at the Wesleyan Hall, where a sheet was suspended over the platform and the projector stood at the front of the balcony. As there was a single performance, the audience were in their seats punctually, and they found nothing odd in being asked to join in a hymn and to listen to announcements about the times of services, the mothers' meeting, and concerts by the choir. The occasion had the amosphere of a village social gathering, a smell of best clothes and lavender water, the waving of handkerchiefs and gloves to greet acquaintances, an agreeable sense of anticipation. The lights went up between the short films, when people gossiped and offered the bags of sweets they had bought on the way there. The operator could be seen changing the reel; this fumbling task completed, he waved importantly to the man who stood near the door by the light-switches.

The proprietor of the first purpose-built cinema, put up in a shopping centre some three miles from the Estate, offered free tea and biscuits (two butter fingers), served to customers in their red plush tip-up seats during the interval by girls dressed as waitresses. When the cups had been cleared away a uniformed man carrying a large syringe walked up the centre gangway spraying a scented mist over the audience's heads. This procedure caused much giggling; people sniffed and tried to guess what the scent was. The cinema, with its waitresses and men in uniforms, was already reaching out to grandeur and assuring the customers of its concern for their welfare. Fears that the cinema could be 'a breeding-ground for epidemics' were widespread. My mother's pleasure in it was marred by the thought of so many people crowded together in the dark with no open windows to be seen; the spraying with what was assumed to be a disinfectant was comforting. Although silent pictures were themselves a wonder, the cinema was even then trying to provide itself with a voice; a highly popular item was 'the singing picture', in which a singer on the screen was accompanied by a record played on a horn gramophone. The words and music of the song could be purchased on the way out.

Before the war ended the cinema had taken on its familiar style with coloured posters, bemedalled commissionaires, a potted tropical plant and a programme culminating in 'the big picture'. The singing picture was dropped; synchronization was difficult. For the first time, working-class families had easily accessible and regular entertainment available to them. Despite the long working hours, one evening a week was spent seeing films; to miss the current picture was a severe deprivation, possibly never to be made good. It became the fashion among teachers, and indeed anyone with intellectual pretensions, to deride the cinema in the same terms that were applied to comics, 'penny dreadfuls', and novelettes—that they diverted the mind from more elevated pursuits and ruined the eyesight. Chaplin's movements had not yet been perceived by highbrows as balletic and Keaton was not recognized as a marvellous mime; their reputations were built on the acclamation of the young, the simple and the uneducated.

People who suppose that mechanized entertainment ousted a lusty culture in the home appear to imagine that the middle class occupied itself with madrigals and string quartets, interspersed with lively conversation, while at a lower level workers and their families gathered round a piano, sang music-hall songs in harmony, and exchanged salty repartee. Neither of these concepts applies to the upper levels of the working class where people were determinedly genteel, daughters had piano and singing lessons and the same drawing-room ballads were demanded and heard respectfully year after year. 'In a Persian Garden', popular in 1896, and 'I'll Sing Thee Songs of Araby', which had been going since 1900, lost none of their charm by repetition over the decades. Invited at a party to sing 'their' song, people would 'render' (to borrow a term much used by the local paper) 'The Galloping Major', 'I Hear You Calling Me', 'When You Come to the End of a Perfect Day', 'Little Grey Home in the West', 'I Love the Moon', or 'Friend o' Mine'. Everybody knew every note and every word and wanted a strict adherence to the familiar interpretation. The nearest they came to vulgarity—it was not very near—was when the inevitable funny uncle sang some of 'his' comic songs; the standard music-hall themes—mothers-in-law, domineering wives, drunken husbands, honeymoons, affected curates, moonlight flits, whitewashing and wallpapering, rotten breakfast-eggs, tough boiling-fowls, debts, pawnbrokers, missed trains—were automatic laughter-raisers. Anecdotal humour was just as stereotyped and unimpaired by repetition. 'Tell us about that time you . . .' someone would inevitably say, and the person appealed to would repeat his account of the mean landlady at Broadstairs, the time the tent fell on him during a camping holiday, his first attempt to ride a bicycle, a series of mishaps when his wife went out and left him to cook his supper. Conversation was scarcely less limited; as soon as it went beyond the bounds of illnesses, deaths, clothes, recipes, prices and children's school reports, one of the women would exclaim in a reproachful little-girl voice: 'Aren't we getting *deep*!' and the man (it was usually a man) would fall silent, reminded that thought and enjoyment were deemed to be incompatible.

Gramophone records came as a welcome interlude. A ten-inch record lasted two and a half minutes; the spring-driven motor had to be wound each time and the volume could not be regulated, so they could not be played as background music. The party was hushed, listened attentively and often asked for several repeats. Everybody was amazed at the lifelike quality of the reproduction; the gramophone did not sound to them as old records do now to an audience accustomed to electronic recording; the ear supplied the natural tone just as the eyes accepted the unnaturalness of black and white photography. That the words were often indistinct bothered nobody either; at concerts and in theatres they were used to not hearing all the words. Whatever the handicaps of acoustic recording, the professional performers' expertise came through, and people who were certainly not unmusical listened with rapture.

The chorus of one of our records ran: 'You'll always find me at the Grand Hotel—or outside, holding horses!' The humour was not then out of date. Ragged boys still hung about pubs, offering to hold horses while the drivers were inside. Within half an hour's gentle cycle ride from the Estate was a rural area where a policeman covered his beat on horseback, elderly ladies drove pony-drawn governess-cars through lanes where the hedges were white with dust, a prosperous architect drove to his office in a brougham. At the foot of steep hills were hoardings, put up by an animal-welfare organization, reading: 'Please give the horse his head going up hill.' Cheap eating-places called themselves cookshops, and boards outside announced: 'Good pull-up for carmen.' Every locality had its smithy, where groups of children loitered watching horses being shod; the smith also repaired boys' iron hoops (girls played with wooden hoops) for a penny. Within the lifetimes of elderly people such scenes could have changed hardly at all. Steam traction-engines were regarded as an undesirable modern invention because of their smoke, noise and speed, and motor-cycles—a few had appeared on the Estate—were considered comic because of the distance the rider had to run before they would start. Motor-buses were objects of amusement too; radiators boiled on a local hill, some drivers carried garden watering-cans which they filled at horse troughs, and sometimes passengers were asked to get out while the bus was driven up the incline in reverse. Traditional engineers viewed motor transport with scepticism, unsure whether the petrol engine was going to last. The speed limit for motor vehicles was twenty miles an hour. Hard-pedalling cyclists were said to be 'scorching' and were widely condemned as a public menace. At lighting-up time police were alert, and local courts could count on a steady revenue from cyclists whose capricious oil-burning rear lamps had gone out. The country still lingered in the Victorian era.

When school broke up in the summer of 1918 our form-master, a reserved uncommunicative man, startled us by saying that he hoped the news would be better by the time we reassembled. The Germans were advancing in what was to be their last great offensive. I think his remark, by the impression it made, must have been the first time we had heard a teacher admit that the war could be going badly for the Allies. The end of hostilities, in the following November, came as a surprise. The newspapers had announced in advance the time of the Armistice but routine was so strong that munitions workers went on their shifts as usual. When the maroons sounded at eleven o'clock my mother was polishing the linoleum—a process she called 'feeding the floor' after an advertisement of a product which 'not only polishes but feeds' the floor, that had appealed to her sense of the absurd. She took off her apron, glanced at her hair in the hall-stand glass, and stepped outside the front door. The sky was over-cast and we shivered in the autumnal chill. A few other housewives emerged, and they waved to each other. Had the Estate had a centre, a market square, a parade, a high street, they might have felt drawn to assemble there, but no focus for spontaneous rejoicing existed. A small party of soldiers straggling along in fours appeared, a familiar sight of men physically and mentally unsuited to army life weighed down with greatcoats, packs and rifles. On seeing the housewives they gave a single cheer and trudged on in the direction of London.

The thudding of the maroons continued, as though somebody had decided to dispose of the remaining stock. My mother returned to feeding the floor, singing at the same time, in the manner of 'darky' concert parties: 'De war am ober now at last, De coloured race am free, De good time coming on so fast, I'se waiting for to see.' It was the only item in her repertoire which appeared to suit the occasion, but it was not all that apt. In no time, with her knuckles pressed against her pale lips and her eyes troubled, she was speculating apprehensively on what would happen next.

At tea-time my father came home; this was, for us, the chief event which marked the day. One might have supposed that the Govern-ment, no longer needing munitions, would have given its workers a paid holiday of a month or so (that would have been only one week for each year of the war), but even in the hour of victory it was in-capable of generosity. It gave them, contemptuously, one Saturday morning off. One of their unions reacted with a telegram to Down-ing Street expressing thanks for this end-of-war holiday of three hours and forty minutes. Paid holidays for industrial workers would have been a dangerous precedent.

By the afternoon of Armistice Day flags appeared from bedroom windows, to my mother's great annoyance. They were untidy, she declared. Probably she classed them with washing hung in the view of the street, a practice respectable housewives abhorred. The next day more flags were displayed, and some houses were festooned with red, white and blue streamers. With unusual enterprise, the village drapery shop was offering a variety of decorations. Ours was the only house not visibly celebrating the victory. Grudgingly she agreed that I should buy a Union Jack, in case some ultra-patriots doubted which side we were on. To her relief neighbours admitted that, although they had put out flags, they thought they made the street look a mess. Even the end of the greatest war in history could not bring them out of their obsessive tidiness. They had the same urge to clear the bunting away as they had to throw out Christmas trees, tear down paper chains and sweep greetings cards from mantelpieces at the first permissible moment. They had an undeviating idea of how a properly-run home should look.

The immediate post-war period was dreary. Spanish 'flu, the last of the great plagues, struck. It was an experience which gave sufferers a life-long dread of influenza. My hair fell out, my nose bled copiously, I had attacks of delirium, in one of which I raved about a law suit, puzzling to my mother until my father, a Dickens addict, came home and identified the case as Jarndyce versus Jarndyce. Once, from the bedroom window, I saw a lorry loaded with coffins. The doctor called daily, although he must have been greatly overworked, and cheerfully told us how many of his patients had died.

The community's industrial heart ceased to beat. The only local product had been lavishly expended and stockpiled against ever more prodigal expenditure. The war to end war being over, it was obvious that gunsmiths and armourers were not going to be in great demand. Some staff would be needed to break up the unwanted ammunition, which task required its own kind of skill, but dedicated specialists felt that producing scrap-metal was a come-down after creating lethal weapons. Some of the unskilled were laid off at once; wearing caps and chokers, they stood around in dejected little groups near their huts—tableaux depicting depression which were to become familiar enough in other parts of the country during the next two decades. The dapper, hard-working Belgian, who had lodged on the

Estate, said goodbyes all round and departed for home to re-establish a small factory. His compatriots, whose behaviour he had deplored, had left without farewells during the previous year, jobs having been found for them somewhere else in England.

It was the end of overtime and income tax, but the beginning of uncertainty. The stories about the multiple buying of fur coats and pianos were soon to be replaced by tales of luxury living on the 'dole' (a term much resented by the unemployed who had supposed that, while working, they were paying insurance premiums—anyone who used the word was sharply corrected). The searchlight station on the Peak was dismantled and the lights of London again lit up the sky to the west; people said the glow was dimmer than before the war—the pre-war days had started to be viewed as a golden age. Lord Kitchener's failure to reappear seemed to go unremarked. The myths, which had infused life with a delicious menace, had peopled the darkness with a shadowy but ineffectual enemy, faded. No one signalled any longer with matches and window blinds. The boy scouts who had once regarded the railway footbridge as a likely objective of an enemy assault were now four years older and perhaps realizing that the assumptions of their families and the local elementary schools that their destiny lay in that huge area of workshops which could be surveyed from the Peak were outdated. Mr Ross, the suspect longterm agent, maintained his fishmonger cover, and seemed unmoved by the fall of the Kaiser's Reich. The yellow-skinned girls no longer crowded the little shops during the dinner-break or paraded with linked arms through the streets; with their poison-coated lungs, their envied wardrobes and their War Savings Certificates they withdrew to regions which regular inhabitants of the Estate could not imagine. A lot of easy business for local shopkeepers went with them, and these slumped into their customary apathy.

One engineering worker who did not try to hang on in a now moribund industry was Hubert, who had hitherto been tied to his job on pain of being called up to the Army if he left it. Did he sense that the heavy industries were in for a slump or did he take the first opportunity of leaving a community where for all time he would be labelled as a bad lot? Did he perhaps foresee that, paradoxically, in a depression the amusement business flourishes? Whatever his motives—and he was uncommunicative both inside and outside his family—he left home to work in a billiards saloon. His mother could scarcely bring herself to utter the words billiards saloon. Yet he felt a compulsion to visit home regularly, as though to assure himself of a base, and he continued to do this after he moved to a fairground and married a gypsy. She must have been the only gypsy who ever entered a house on the Estate. She carried her baby tied to her in a shawl, as if to leave the other arm free for a basket of clothes pegs. Hubert wore a rakish cap and a choker. When he left the house with his wife and child he never looked round to show his face to the watchers concealed behind the curtains. The only sentiment ever expressed about him was horror. 'It would be better for his mother if he didn't come to see her,' was the most usual remark. No one speculated about what Hubert's wife's family thought of her choice of a husband, about whether he was a welcome recruit to the fairground community or regarded as a refugee deserter from that hard-faced race which opened front doors so warily and closed them so promptly and so firmly.

Now should have been the time for the fulfilment of those dreams, nourished by *The Smallholder* and lavishly distributed government pamphlets on rabbit-breeding and apple-growing, of an exodus to the country. Only one of the considerable number who had talked so wistfully of going on the land did so. He was a foreman in the T.N.T. filling factory who, in moments of depression, felt himself doomed and in optimistic phases hoped that constant fresh air would save his lungs. While his fellows had been dreaming of an idyllic rural existence, he had been calculating how many rolls of wire netting enclosed what area and deciding which oil pump to buy. His announcement that he had bought a farm in Norfolk was met with incredulity, as though farming had never before been mentioned as a post-war occupation. The rest were immobile. Apprehensive though they were about their futures, habit and caution tied them to their jobs, homes, gardens and allotments; the discovery of a goldfield in the neighbouring county would not have tempted them to move.

❧ 11 ❧

Ain't We Had Fun!

The characteristic picture of the 1920s (Ma Meyrick's nightclubs, Taggs Island, Lady Cunard's parties, Bright Young Things, cocktails, tango teas, Mah-Jongg) seemed as remote to most people then as it does to readers now. But 'the wireless' opened up the world, displaced the vicar as the pronunciation authority, robbed the men of their evening excuse for going to the station to check the time, provided frequent news bulletins which became compulsive listening, and introduced into dull households the nightly joy of the Savoy Orpheans. Solid-tyred open motor-coaches offered excursions to the Kentish hopfields and other destinations not conveniently accessible by train; people were amazed that a round trip of sixty miles was possible in half a day. The local barber made a decision which he was to regret for the rest of his working life—he refused to cut women's hair. Crossword puzzles appeared; I actually heard a Labour M.P. denounce these for taking the workers' minds off their grievances.

Veils of reticence were cautiously parted. An evening class in psychology enrolled curious members who were very solemn about the subject in case people suspected their motives; mention of Freud aroused apprehensions that the speaker was about to say something unsuitable for mixed company. Jane, always in the van of progress, made occasional vague and reverent references to Marie Stopes. People who claimed to have read Michael Arlen's *The Green Hat* were enigmatically tight-lipped about its theme as though they had been initiated into a mystery. It was fashionable to pretend to be 'naughty', a pose which deceived parsons and some parents into thinking that naughtiness was in fact going on. Girls smoked miniature gold-tipped cigarettes, carried walking-sticks and strode in an unladylike manner. None was jauntier than Molly and her close friend, Vera. Molly's mother found the attachment of these two reassuring; so long as they were together they could come to no harm. 'My Molly isn't interested in young men,' she would say proudly, grimacing at the idea of girls who were. But the girls worked hard at creating the impression that they were 'fast'.

[142]

Their hair was bobbed and they dabbed powder puffs round their faces in public while gazing intently into handbag mirrors. To have used lipstick then would have been going too far. In mid-calf costumes they marched rapidly across the heath, swinging their sticks vigorously, chatting incessantly and laughing ostentatiously. The sticks, of course, were an attention-getting accessory, but while attracting glances the girls were also in flight, protected by each other's company. The acquisition of young men would have disturbed the set-up. At parties they sat on a sofa with their arms round each other. One a soprano and the other a contralto, they sang duets—'O that we two were sleeping, In our graves 'neath the churchyard sod.' When the mood changed they sang, with roguish smiles, 'I want a boy, I want a great big wonderful boy.' Daringly, at a Christmas party where port, sherry and ginger wine were circulating, they sang a parody of a popular drawing-room ballad: 'I passed by your window when you were undressed, You took off your camisole and stood in your vest. . . .' Rather taken aback, Mrs Perry was later heard to speculate on where they had picked this up as though they had contracted an infectious disease, but there was no evidence that the girls' actions were other than irreproachable. At socials, where men were always in a minority, they danced together, dipping and swaying, pleated skirts swirling, and smiling into each other's eyes. In the autumn, when the days shortened but the evenings remained warm, couples made for the dark woods— the only place where they could rely on privacy. The two girls signed on for evening classes in French and shorthand.

They were by no means the only female pair following this kind of routine. Young women enjoyed a new-found independence because they could earn money. The depression did not affect them as it did men; some kind of employment was always available to them. They could pay for their clothes, take themselves to cinemas and go on holiday together. But they were far from independent of their parents' approval; acquaintanceships with the opposite sex caused mothers to become sour and families sarcastic. If a girl's closest friend was another girl, she was respectable and left in peace.

Sometimes a pair of girls would acquire boyfriends, and then they found it useful to let it appear that their friendship remained on its old basis. They would go out together, separate for the evening, and meet again to come home—a procedure giving rise to less stress than introducing a male acquaintance to their families. In a neighbourhood where casual dropping in for drinks, spontaneous parties, last-minute invitations were unknown, where a sociably-inclined person could live for twenty years without entering more than six other houses, visits could only be planned, and the expectation of visitors involved a neurotic frenzy of dusting and polishing. Boys and girls were acutely aware of the implications of inviting someone of the opposite sex to their homes; the ground had to be diplomatically prepared and a time appointed, and then the new-comer was scrutinized as a possible—indeed, likely—son or daughter-in-law. Family pressure often resulted in boys and girls who had never moved outside a narrow circle entering prematurely into en-gagements which lasted for years (while they 'saved up') and were marked by periodic explosions of temper, intervals of 'not speaking' and by a barely controlled irritability at other times. Or they carried on a clandestine relationship, which was difficult without such facilities as telephones and cars, and also liable to cause bad temper. In either case, they ultimately got married at a stage where, in more liberated circles, they would have been getting divorced.

Attitudes had scarcely altered since before the war. The only man who wanted to change partners was condemned in terms no less forth-right than those which had been applied to Hubert's conduct. He was Mr Wyatt, who had been expected to emerge from his Washing-ton funk hole soon after the Armistice. Important matters, however, detained him, and he returned evasive answers to his wife's sugges-tions that she and her sons should join him. But it was only retro-spectively that his answers were seen to have been evasive; at the time of receipt they had been interpreted as encouraging, and the family had become convinced that either he would arrive home soon or they would go to Washington. When he finally wrote that he meant to stay there and did not intend his family to join him, that he was making financial provision for them and wanted a divorce, his wife was incredulous. Shortly after the letter came she was read-ing it to my mother, and making such comments as: 'Those are not Jim's words. Somebody is standing over him and dictating them.' He must know, she said, that for Catholics divorce was out of the ques-tion, and even now she was on her way to see the priest. For what seemed a very long time the Wyatt case dominated conversation. Some explanation had to be found for his aberrant behaviour. It was agreed that he had 'got into the clutches of a harpy', but why had he allowed himself to do so? The most favoured reason was that he was a Welshman. I doubt whether, in these discussions, any statistics were produced of the divorce and wife-desertion rates in Wales compared with the rest of the United Kingdom, but the popular view of the Welsh was that they were promiscuous and my elders seemed satisfied that the puzzle had been solved.

Although no Bright Young Things emerged, young people collectively known as Youth (as in Youth demands, Youth will no longer tolerate, and so on) did. Teenagers were then unknown, and adolescence had been regarded as a tiresome phase to be got through as quickly as possible; those enduring it were ignored, slapped down or laughed at. I first learnt that one did not have to be apologetic about being young from Miss Susan Lawrence, a prominent Labour politician, who said in a lecture that the post-war generation was quite unlike any preceding generation; its eyes had been opened, it was determined to avoid its elders' mistakes which had resulted in the war, and political parties would in future have to listen to it. Jane warmly endorsed this, and assumed an expression of listening intently whenever any of us spoke. Youth's right to be heard was established, although the period when one could claim to be young was quite brief; infancy did not, as now, extend to the age of twenty-five and, for anyone professing to be a research student, many years beyond that. Youth movements proliferated and showed that they could form committees, sub-committees and joint committees with no less facility than their seniors. Their members were invariably in high spirits and anticipating a breakthrough—the peacetime equivalent of the decisive cavalry charge—to a new social order by the time they were grown up.

The youth movement was only one symptom of the political mood which gripped the Estate. The district had escaped the grimmer aspects of the post-war depression. Optimism prevailed. Researchers may read the political manifestos, pamphlets and speeches of the decade, and study the biographies of politicians, without receiving any impression of the degree of euphoria which brought in Labour votes. No reporters attended the meetings in tiny halls and elementary schools or eavesdropped on committees gathered in somebody's front room. It was in such humble surroundings that the spirit of 'the movement' was expressed without inhibition. Speakers did not need to worry about reading their speeches in print; nobody cared whether what they said was approved party policy; central office never had to issue disclaimers. Audiences had not come to hear expositions of conference resolutions. After a boring, and possibly humiliating day in the workshop, or lonely hours of polishing, mending and cooking, they wanted emotion, uplift, hope, something to take them out of themselves, to restore their self-esteem. Participation in meetings had, especially for those who held some office, a therapeutic value; nobodies during the day were somebodies in the evening; the bewildering structure of the outside world was simplified; daydreams became certainties.

Audiences must not be imagined as wearing the tense expressions of actors in scenes where a crowd is listening to a revolutionary orator; nobody muttered or shook a fist. Comfortable-looking pipe-smoking men sat back in their chairs; women, mostly overweight, knitted, passed bags of sweets, or just gazed maternally at the speaker. Alert young men and women, the kind who attended evening classes and drama societies, sat in groups, ready to laugh at any witticism. Nobody was attending as a solemn duty or out of a burning sense of injustice; it was an evening's diversion, a social occasion. It was fun.

Speakers would give their talks a semblance of topicality by referring to current themes—the aftermath of the war, unemployment, the Geddes axe, falling wages, the profits of big business, trusts and combines, the machinations of bankers; behind all these phenomena, it was implied even when not specifically stated, lurked the same group of international capitalists. Ireland was usually mentioned so that the British Government's use of the Black and Tans could be recalled. Such subjects were the lead-in to a discourse which sounded like a revivalist sermon and was about as difficult to analyse. Having arrived at this state, most orators needed no notes; whatever title their lecture had been given, whatever the occasion, the text scarcely varied over the years. They were like music-hall performers who, before the coming of radio, could tour the country with one act for their entire professional lives. The miseries of the industrial revolution were deplored. The descendants of the wicked mill-owners were the present-day Tories and Liberals, whose end was now in sight. The immoral capitalist system was entering its final stage of dissolution. A curious puritanism often emerged in this context; the capitalist system and the Devil might have been interchangeable; both sought to lure the faithful from the path of salvation by such diversions as horse-racing, alcohol, the cinema, modern dancing and popular fiction. The speakers themselves, of course, did not make this comparison, but agnostics and Primitive Methodists were at one in advocating austerity. The constantly repeated assertion was that the Labour Party was based on morality instead of self-seeking; it was not a political party like the other two and it must remain uncontaminated by them. When it attained power it must not tinker with the capitalist system (hence nobody present, including the speaker himself, need bother to understand such transient features of it as the gold standard, the trade balance, Bank rate) but must abolish it. This summary scarcely does justice to some of the perorations, which envisaged a not far distant time when, in the words of their secular hymn, 'all the earth is paradise'.

The placidity, the amiability and cosiness might, one would have thought, have caused visiting speakers to fear that their eloquence had failed. Such misgivings would have been unnecessary. Everyone was completely and unquestioningly committed to the Labour movement. Very occasionally the deep feelings surfaced. One girl broke off her engagement because her fiancé, an alien to the Estate, voted Conservative. Mrs Baxter, the hatless suffragette, suffered a nervous breakdown after Ramsay MacDonald was defeated in a by-election. Her reaction was extreme, but many others adored MacDonald, a handsome and courageous man and perhaps, apart from Lloyd George, the best orator of his day. He was the leader, and if they did not always understand what he was talking about, no shadow crossed their minds. They accepted the message, whatever it was.

It is remarkable that so little genuine debate went on at those local meetings. People simply wanted to be told what it was proper to think; it never occurred to them that they could put in a bid for what they in their hearts wanted. With virtually no discussion (an anti-nationalization resolution would have been unthinkable) they committed themselves to the principle of state control. Yet when they talked among themselves they did not say that their hope for the future was to work in mammoth state-owned factories; most of the men had done that for years. The experience could not have taught them that the Government was a generous employer. Bank holidays were their only paid time off, they had no security and no pensions, and when they retired, after probably fifty years' service, they received their final week's wages and a printed octavo slip containing a few formal words of thanks over the facsimile signature of the current secretary of state. G. D. H. Cole's advocacy of guild socialism never reached their ears, except perhaps as an aside in the course of a lecture; if they could have considered it without fear of being unorthodox many of them might have discovered that they were guild socialists, even though inarticulate ones, without knowing it. What about their dreams of owning small farms or managing country pubs? Suppose that, through some misunderstanding by the local secretary, G. K. Chesterton had appeared on the platform of The Hall and that he had expounded (without mentioning that it was called Distributivism and not Socialism) his policy of the widespread ownership of property. Surely it would have sounded more congenial to them, more consistent with their traditions and habits of thought, than would the doctrines of Sidney and Beatrice Webb.

But the formula had been found; further thought was unnecessary. State ownership would end immoral private profit, the waste inevitable in competition, the exploitation of labour and the consumer, social inequality, poverty, crime (the result of poverty), war (caused by capitalists struggling for raw materials and markets), and labour disputes (the workers would never strike against themselves). To objections raised elsewhere, by opponents of nationalization, that state management would be inefficient, speakers had a crushing retort. Look, they would say, at the Post Office. Where, throughout the whole range of private enterprise, can you find an organization so efficient and cheap? It was a telling argument; the Post Office was everybody's pride, a symbol of reliability and integrity; its postmen, striding through urban streets or cycling along farm tracks in the dark of a winter morning, giving their familiar double knock, were everybody's friends, and living symbols of a benevolent state. They enjoyed an enviable status; they were Civil Servants, immune from the hazards of most other employment, settled for life, pensionable.

Civil Service conditions were a powerful lure. To attain security, boys and girls were induced to jettison whatever dreams they had of adventure and fun in favour of routine, clean, spirit-cramping jobs. Entry to the Service was by no means assured to those who made the decision. The examination subjects looked simple but, with many thousands competing for a few hundred posts, standards were exacting. The 'Civil Service hand' had to be acquired—flowing, legible handwriting. Orthography had to be taken seriously; intending applicants studied lists of difficult words, watched out for alternative spellings and the most commonly misspelt words, drilled themselves to distinguish between words ending in 'able' and 'ible', felt anxiety about which words double the consonant with a suffix. 'Tots' caused headaches; columns of figures had to be 'totted up' not only accurately but very quickly. Friends were invited to time applicants, who sat in an agony of concentration, pencils moving up and down six-column numbers, lips moving. Speed was required in all subjects as well as perfection. The précis and the essay were regarded as relatively easy, but these, too, allowed no time for brooding. The examiners projected an image of government departments supervised by relentless overseers with stop-watches and staffed by clerks frantically doing lengthy sums, providing an instant précis of bulky documents, producing in faultless handwriting drafts, memos and correspondence, without a pause for thought. Candidates who completed this exhausting obstacle-race with a minimum of errors were privileged to enter the lower grades where, admittedly, they found the pace of work less hectic than the examination papers suggested.

Dorothy, sister of the delinquent Hubert, was among the fortunate elect. She was a shorthand-typist, a term which in those days was applied only to the skilled. She needed the same standards of literacy as did other Civil Servants; there would have been no tolerance for girls who could not read their shorthand outlines, who made grammatical and spelling mistakes, and who were unacquainted with titles and forms of address. The art and craft of typing involved the neat spacing of headlines, a pleasing display of the text, tabulating, the invisible correction of errors even in the carbon copies. Typists regarded themselves as ladies and assumed a certain status both in their offices and among their acquaintances.

Her early years in the Civil Service were reasonably happy, but then came a change. Every morning she left for the office in a state of apprehension, cried in her bedroom in the evening, moped about, saw herself as facing years of misery until she drew her pension. The cause was the institution of a typing-pool. Efficiency experts had appeared and pointed out that shorthand-typists allocated to individual offices were not all consistently occupied throughout every day. It was an argument which looked good on paper to anyone who viewed the matter from above rather than from below. The experts failed to consider that a girl working permanently in a department acquired its specialist vocabulary, knew the names of the people and institutions it dealt with, could find her way through its files, understood its officials' individual whims. Perhaps above all they ignored the female's propensity to personalize organizations and to mother her colleagues.

Snatched out of her familiar office, her daytime home, Dorothy found herself taking dictation from strange men on unfamiliar subjects. One man talked with a pipe between his teeth, one spoke with a marked provincial accent, one mumbled while gazing at the ceiling. The least intelligible were the most inclined to snap when asked to repeat what they had said. Given time she would have learnt to cope with even the most difficult of them, but the way she was shuttled about a large building gave her no chance. The efficiency men had turned a contented girl into an unhappy one.

When they carried out their work-studies and made their recommendations it was certainly with no ill intent. They would have been surprised, perhaps even moved, to know about that young woman sobbing in her bedroom. If, before taking up their jobs, they had had to do a couple of years' stint as shorthand-typists themselves, had experienced the anxiety of reducing false starts, repetitions, parentheses, throat-clearings and nose-blowings to lucid sentences, the agony of cramp and backache, they might have viewed more tolerantly the spectacle of a girl getting on with her knitting while, having finished her typing, she waited for another spell of dictation.

Gradually Dorothy and her colleagues calmed down, not because they adapted themselves to the pool but because the pool accommodated itself to them. The work-rationalizers had got their scheme accepted and had moved on to upset other departments. Diagrams at their headquarters showed the pool in operation, and for their kind it is diagrams and charts which constitute reality. Back at the scene of their reform, however, a subtle modification slowly occurred. Without any official notification a further reform was instituted, which avoided the bother of telephoning the pool and waiting for the girl and her notebook to arrive. Shorthand-typists, while still belonging to the pool, could now be allocated to departments on permanent loan. Dorothy was back in her old department again.

Young male office-workers tended to be apologetic about the careers they had embarked on. Unaware that they were part of a general switch to white-collar occupations, they felt that they were breaking a tradition and betraying their boyhood assumptions. Boys of this class found it hard to imagine what *men* did in offices.

Implanted in them was the conviction that a man ought to know how machinery worked; that was the only real knowledge. Fathers felt it a duty to prepare sons for life by taking every opportunity to demonstrate what made things tick. My father took pleasure in explaining the movement of a watch. Steam-rollers and traction-engines occasioned impromptu lectures. Our trips on the Belle steamers never omitted a visit to the engine-room, for me an almost frightening experience of shining metal, shuddering movement, a massive pulse, a smell of steam and hot oil. My father was thrilled by the gleaming perfection, the rhythm, the controlled power which turned the huge paddles. Bells rang, his eyes lit expectantly, and he smiled at me, trying to convey his pleasure, as the engines slowed and the beat changed. An overalled man walked slowly along a platform, occasionally leaned over a railing to touch some part with the long spout of an oil can, and he always approached us for a chat. 'I would hate not knowing how a thing works,' my father often said to me when I was small. At the time he said it I suppose he knew how virtually all machines worked, or could have understood them after some observation. The emergence, in the 1920s, of 'the wireless' depressed him, avid listener though he soon became, because he realized that technically he was being left behind. He always imagined himself stranded, like Robinson Crusoe, unable to call on the services of bicycle-repairers, gas-fitters, plumbers, sewing-machine agents, watchmakers. Although he would not have attempted to do these men's jobs, he felt uneasy unless he knew how to do them. Anything with working parts was poised to cause him a set-back at any moment. When I acquired a typewriter he took a long look at it and asked: 'What do you do when it breaks down?'

Stringent entrance-requirements resulted in the employment of many young people who were too intelligent for their jobs. Not all were, like Dorothy, willing to settle for a quiet life. Much of their spare time was spent in seeking the satisfaction they lacked during the day. Seized by a craving for culture, as evening students they flocked eagerly to those London County Council schools which, as day pupils, they had left no less eagerly a few years previously. Or they dominated classes run by the Workers' Education Association. In their neat outfits—it was fashionable to be clean and well-groomed—and wearing horn-rimmed spectacles, flipping over the pages of notebooks as they wrote at professional speed, they bore no resemblance to the workers envisaged by the Association's founders.

Throughout the twenties William Henry observed the Estate from time to time and was unmoved. He sat through a good many meetings but he never lost an air of total detachment. Any event was to him no more than so many column inches. Speakers and audiences would have been surprised to know that this amiable, self-effacing man regarded himself as the most important person present. Somewhere—I cannot believe that he had read the work from which the quotation came—he had picked up a sentence by Carlyle: 'Burke said there were Three Estates in Parliament; but, in the Reporters' Gallery yonder, there sat a *Fourth Estate* more important far than they all.' Writing impeccable Pitman's, he had sat in that gallery and felt superior to the entire Cabinet. What he felt for the lesser speakers who appeared at local meetings he made plain as soon as he sat himself at the Press table.

While the chairman was making his introductory remarks and the speaker was getting started, William Henry—using every abbreviation known to printers—was writing his opening paragraph lengthwise on an octavo pad. The practice of tearing an attention-catching sentence from the body of the speech and starting with that was one be scorned; if sub-editors played about with his copy he did not mind so long as they refrained from reducing the number of lines. He stated where and when the meeting was held, under whose auspices (one of his favourite words), the name of the chairman who ably presided and the name of the speaker, who was not infrequently accorded a rousing reception. Then he addressed a buff octavo envelope to his editor and started his notetaking, continuing until he had exactly enough for a column. After that, because he was transcribing his notes, he was deaf to anything the speaker might say. It must have been deflating for the speaker when the reporter assembled the wad of sheets, tapped them smartly on the table before fitting them into the envelope, licked the envelope and the stamp, replaced his glasses in their case with a loud snap, pushed his chair back noisily, slowly put his coat on, picked up the envelope and his hat, and walked out with his normal tread. On these occasions he looked cosily self-contained, secure in his power to put—or not to put—words into print. People looked round as he pushed the door open and let it swing to after him.

For years he had bought magazines; they were not an extra-vagance but an investment. He clipped articles, classified and indexed them, and from them he bred fresh articles which he sold to the then numerous small cheaply-produced periodicals 'for home reading'. One series he wrote was about workers whose labours we take for granted. 'How often', one of them began, 'as we sit in a cosy armchair before a glowing fire, do we pause to think of the miner toiling in the bowels of the earth?' So far as one editor was concerned, William Henry had struck a rewarding seam. As we sat comfortably at home we did not think of deep-sea fishermen hauling in the catch on ice-covered decks, of weary train-drivers on rocking footplates peering through the gloom, of shepherds on bleak moorland, of policemen on windy street corners, of bakers starting work before dawn, of milkmen, lighthouse-keepers, sewage-workers, postmen—the series ran on to include the men who made the cosy armchair, wove the carpet, built the house. Readers whose social conscience he awakened must have felt their heads spinning, but such a result would have astonished him, as he attached no meaning to what he wrote. The poet of whom Humbert Wolfe said: 'A primrose by the river's brim, Was one-and-six a line to him, And it was nothing more,' belonged to the same school of magazine contributors as did William Henry.

He also turned out sketches in a facetious style then still in fashion but now encountered only in staff journals, school magazines and letters to local newspapers. The writer assumed the role of a whimsi-cal, fastidious observer who regarded the contemporary world with amused disdain. 'A charming young lady whose charms would have been even greater had she not sought to enhance them by a liberal use of rouge and powder.' 'My ears were assailed by the strident cacophony of so-called popular music.' 'He arrived on an alarming and noisy contraption known colloquially as a motor-bike.' 'I was accosted by a person of somewhat bedraggled appearance who emerged from an insalubrious-looking alley.' 'An assortment of highly obnoxious effluvia greeted my nostrils as I reluctantly entered the premises.' Phrases and sentences like this came so readily to him that he never groped around while writing an article; a writer's self-doubting agonies were unknown to him. Headlines sometimes briefly delayed his output, because he thought nothing was so eye-catching as alliteration. 'Apt alliteration's artful aid,' he would remark with a chuckle. 'Cautious Councillors Cancel Contract.' He tried it out aloud. 'President Presents Prizes.' That one came up for regular use as he felt it could not be bettered. If he had a favourite, it was 'Doubting Delegates Demand Details'.

At the end of the decade he gave up reporting and retired, as he put it, to 'slippered ease'.

A decade of peace did not restore the Estate's Sabbath decorum. An obligation to go to church, or at least to look as though one had been to church, no longer existed. Changing fashions had deprived the parade across the heath of its dignity. Not even Mrs Baxter, released from a mental hospital where the treatment had calmed her down but failed to cure her passionate fixation on Ramsay MacDonald, attracted glances; other women were hatless and walking freely. Buses ran along the road where the promenaders had once spread themselves, and some of the passing cars contained women who a few years previously had, on religious grounds, refused to allow their children to ride bicycles on Sundays. God, it had been revealed, was placated by attendance at early Communion, after which the day could be devoted to secular pleasures.

But even if religious observance was declining, God was still to be reckoned with. The case of Molly Perry demonstrated that. Despite families' obsessive secrecy, the revelation of what was going on spread beyond the immediate circle of relatives; it was as though the reverberations of the emotions aroused could not be contained within one small house.

Molly and Vera, devoted to one another with a passion which might have caused raised eyebrows in a different milieu, were the pride of their parents and, presumably, the despair of would-be seducers. They went regularly to Communion and evensong, had steady jobs in placid offices, contributed generously to household expenses, and in their spare time pursued unwaveringly their innocent routine of socials, whist drives and evening classes. Sometimes Mrs Perry seemed to feel that some explanation of their celibacy, apart from their ladylike indifference to the other sex, was called for, and then she would say: 'The men Molly and Vera would have married were killed in the war.' An entire male generation had been screened during those four years, the best selected for sacrifice, and the remainder could not aspire to marry these young women, who could thus, with dignity, mourn the suitors who had never appeared and remain in the parental home. It was, from the elders' viewpoint, a comfortable arrangement. When a threat to its continuance arose, and in a manner which shattered the whole concept of her daughter's nature, Mrs Perry was aghast. The episode of Molly's gesture of independence when she fled from domestic service had not been forgotten; that she should win a second rebellion was unthinkable. Mrs Perry decided to stake her family's stability on one confrontation. If Molly was not a hopelessly lost soul, the risk was small.

She chose a time when her husband and son were absent. Molly was upstairs changing to go out for the evening. When the young woman, then in her late twenties, came down to the living-room (which, after local fashion, they called the kitchen—a large black-leaded range was set into the wall below a high mantelpiece) her mother eyed her. Was she dressed like that merely to go out with Vera? Was that an unfamiliar, and more pungent, perfume? Had her expression changed and was she, as she pulled on her gloves and remarked that she would be back at the usual time, avoiding her mother's eyes? To an unprejudiced observer Molly would have looked a simple suburban girl; to her mother she was a Jezebel.

Hitherto the letters on the older woman's lap had been concealed by the table. Now she placed them on the shiny oilcloth cover. The daughter immediately recognized them, and hostilities opened spontaneously.

The verbal conflict was conducted with that viciousness characteristic of family rows: whatever the proximate cause, feelings are fuelled by the accumulated resentments of years of enforced proximity; every past slight is suddenly present. Molly's capacity for self-righteous indignation was no less than her mother's. Choosing to ignore what the correspondence revealed, she attacked, protesting that her mother had been prying into her handbag.

'God led me to your handbag, Molly!' Mrs Perry retorted.

Molly might have inquired how many times God had led her to that handbag without rewarding her inquisitiveness. She could have followed up this parry with a threat to leave home at once. Not only did Molly contribute generously to household expenses, but she advanced loans whenever her mother had indulged in some relatively extravagant purchase. Mrs Perry's weakness was impulse-buying. While she would never have run seriously into debt, she was tempted by bargains and thus not infrequently ran short of housekeeping money. 'The Lord will provide,' she said on such occasions. The Lord did—out of Molly's pay packet, and without making any stipulations as to interest or repayment. If Molly had removed herself to a flat, as she could well have afforded to do, Mrs Perry would have had to reduce her standard of living and restrain her impulses.

But after that initial retort, Molly's defence weakened. She was handicapped by believing in a God who observed her every action and by whom she would be judged. At that moment, in God's presence, she could not plead her mother's meanness and spite. She knew that to have an *affaire* with a married man was wicked. The screaming went on, however, until both parties were hoarse and exhausted.

No fundamentalist chapel preacher could have expressed horror more volubly than Mrs Perry; no betrayed woman could have screamed and wept with more abandon than Molly; yet in the one matter which might have seemed crucial—whether Molly had 'fallen'—reticence was observed. Except insofar as it was implied in references to sin and disgrace, direct mention of that subject by mother and daughter was taboo. Among those who became acquainted with the scandal the talk was freer, going as far as the assumption that an illegitimate baby was the inevitable consequence. Marie Stopes had preached in vain where they were concerned; a wayward girl paid the penalty and that was that.

Time was to show that the ultimate disgrace was not to be incurred. That could not have been concealed from the vicar, and it was Mrs Perry's great concern that he should hear no whisper of this incredible episode. Had he done so, Mrs Perry would never have felt able to approach the altar, let alone to arrange the flowers on it, again. Nor could he have been expected to drink a cup of tea in that house of shame. Although he no longer walked through the streets blessing the children, as Mr Charlesworth had done, and dropping in to tea and biscuits with ordinary members of his congregation, he still called on the small circle of church helpers. Mrs Perry would have felt banished to outer darkness if these visits had ceased.

As more details became available, the drama acquired a new twist. The man was a regular Army major and several years Molly's senior, clearly a Sir Jasper to whose flattering attentions an innocent maiden had all but succumbed. By now she was slowly on the way to re-instatement; the accepted version of the story was that she had been tempted but had not—could not have—surrendered.

Not every revolt succeeds. The advance to freedom encounters its set-backs. Molly promised never to see the major again. More than

that, she associated her lapse with the progressive views she had
picked up on the Estate. 'There's something peculiar about those
people,' she declared in a moment of decision. 'I want nothing more
to do with them.' The peculiar people were the Estate's high-minded
progressives, those propagandists for a new moral world. By her tone
they might have been wife-swappers, advocates of free love. If she
was asserting that but for their influence she would not have
strayed, she had grievously misunderstood them.

Absolution was not to be obtained from the vicar, but it was to
the church that she ran for shelter. It was a pity that the vicar never
knew how the church had triumphed over its secular rival. He might
have been encouraged to try to retain the allegiance of, among others,
those of the choir who were no longer able to reach the high notes.
When they drifted away from the church it was because they ob-
jected not to its investments in slum property, its silence on social
questions, or its identification with what would now be called the
Establishment, but its failure to teach its doctrine at an adult level.
While secular organizations were offering classes in such subjects as
political theory, economics, history and philosophy, and requiring
their part-time students to read set books and write essays, the local
religious teaching for adults was scarcely above the Sunday school
level. No publication entering Estate houses was so banal as the
parish magazine; its messages, from the vicar's to the archbishop's,
revealed no glimpse of the wisdom one might have expected from
men whose lives were spent reflecting on eternal truths. No professional theologian was ever invited to the locality to lecture. No
vicar ever compiled a reading list of religious works. Yet the clergy
were not stupid men; surely they could have produced some evidence
that their minds were working. Were they content to be surrounded
by feminine tea-makers and flower-arrangers? Much concerned as
they still were with heathens overseas, they ignored the growing
number at home.

❧ 12 ❧

Twilight in the Woods

The programme at the annual Grand Fête and Gala had changed very little by 1929. The rustic shed, the simple stage, the marquee had not been displaced by anything more elaborate. The silver prize band, instead of marching there at the head of a procession, had arrived in what was then called a charabanc; changed fashions in dancing at public events had caused the deletion of The Lancers from its repertoire (without the discipline imposed by the M.C. and Jane there would have been hopeless confusion) and foxtrots and one-steps dominated the programme. Nigger minstrels were out of fashion. Nothing very sparkling had taken their place but, despite the wireless, the audience still crowded the benches. People were less formally dressed; that heavy garment, more suitable for winter than summer and curiously termed a sports jacket, had been adopted by many of the men, and hats were going out. One man, who during the meeting sat on the platform among the committee, wore an ordinary shirt without a collar to proclaim himself a proletarian and a Communist. He represented a viewpoint alien to the Estate, where it had been customary to demonstrate one's prosperity and respectability rather than one's poverty and slovenliness. He came from outside, from that grey region in the middle distance between the Peak and St Paul's, as did a majority of the people listening to the band, looking at the flowers and crowding the refreshment hut. The occasion was no longer a cosy, local affair. Trams had destroyed the Estate's comparative isolation.

The invaders were more restless than the Estate residents; their children ran about, collided with people, scuffled with one another, and were shouted at by their parents; the refreshment hut resounded with querulous voices. 'They make such a commotion,' locals remarked, recalling the garden-party tranquillity of the time when they had the woods to themselves. Walter and Jane, as they made their unobtrusive appearance, were a reminder of those more formal days, he in a carefully pressed light-grey suit, a stiff white collar and a felt hat which looked as though he was wearing it for the first time; she, gloved and hatted, in an unfashionably long rustling dress under a shimmering light coat with a flowered pattern. If they came into their own on that day, it was late in the evening, after the crowd had departed for their London-bound trams, and when only Estate residents—Walter's original co-operative colonists—remained.

Dusk touched the woods with mystery. The coloured lights were left on, while exhibitors removed their vases, potted plants and trays of vegetables, and workmen stacked trestle-tables and benches. Spectacles, necklaces and ornamental buttons reflected the illuminations. Birds in the surrounding trees made restless noises, bats swooped erratically over the open space, midges swarmed. In the distance could be heard receding calls of goodnight, and the decelerating and accelerating note of trams, those nauseating carriages of the workers, as they approached and left stops. Familiar faces in the dusk looked warm and friendly. Moved by a communal feeling, little groups drew together, like a family left to itself after an over-long party, like residents of a holiday resort when the last of the season's visitors has gone. Somebody yawned, apologized, laughed. Somebody inevitably said: 'Sunday tomorrow. You can have a nice lie-in.'

No garden-party bitchiness enlivened the conversation; no malicious innuendoes were uttered to send the participants home in a mood of giggling superiority. Such talk would have been unthinkable in the presence of Walter and Jane, who never questioned anyone's motives and who supposed that everyone was as sincere as they were. An outsider might have noted with surprise an assumption, made by everyone in those little groups, that whatever they engaged in, whether attending lectures and classes, participating in country dancing, theatricals or visits to art galleries, they were advancing a cause. Nothing was undertaken for its own sake. Languages were studied to promote international understanding, any activity remotely connected with the arts was a preparation for life in the new social order—their ingenuity in finding selfless reasons was boundless.

This attitude was projected on to the Estate; it was a staging post on the way to the millennium. The Estate into which they were about to emerge as, still talking, they made their way to the gate, was less real to them than the phantom Estate in which their faith was, they were convinced, so soundly invested.